WHAT EVERY PARENT NEEDS TO KNOW ABOUT EATING DISORDERS

TONJA H. KRAUTTER, PSY.D., L.C.S.W.

PUBLISHED BY FASTPENCIL, INC.

I dedicate this book to the many patients I have worked with through the years who have suffered from eating disorders. It has been both an honor and a privilege to have worked with these amazing individuals in their journey through treatment and recovery. Their courage, strength and commitment to overcome this devastating illness is an inspiration to all persons who believe they will never get better. They are proof that with proper treatment, a good support system, and the willingness and motivation to change, recovery is not only possible, it is probable. Thank you for sharing your journey with me.

୭ଏ

Acknowledgements

I am a Practicing Clinical Psychologist who finds great meaning in helping others. I feel honored and privileged to work in the mental health field. In addition, I am a mother who finds great meaning in raising two precious children. Both my family and my career are priorities in my life. I feel blessed to have created a balance between them.

The identification and understanding of the development of an eating disorder can leave a family feeling frustrated, frightened, confused, and defeated. My greatest hope in writing this book is to provide knowledge about eating disorders to all families who are currently raising pre-teen or teenage children in our society today. We are witnessing first hand a dramatic cultural phenomenon among our youth circled around disordered eating and distorted body image. By acknowledging this shift, we are able to gain a better understanding of the complexities involved and offered the opportunity to help our children in both positive and healthy ways.

I would like to acknowledge the contributions of several people, without whom, I would not have completed this book.

To my incredible editor, Stacey Paris McCutcheon. Thank you for your interest and commitment to this book project. You inspired me to finish this book and start some new ones. You are wonderful!

To my dedicated readers, Dr. Fawn Powers, Dr. James Lock, and Grace Shih. Thank you for your time and effort in reviewing this book. It is an honor and privilege to have your support and guidance.

To my good friend, Steve O'Deegan, for his hard work and commitment to the finalized product.

To the many people who supported me in my efforts and convinced me that this book was a must read for parents who are raising pre-teens and teenagers in society today: Andrea Ancha, Anthony Atwell, Rebecca Powers, Gale Uhl, Veronica Saleh, Ann Martini, Betsy Cregger, Judith Siegel, Larry Gibson (R.I.P.), Christina Halsey, Tom Miller, Dennis Champion, Anne Takahashi, James Cosse (R.I.P.), Carole Brennan, Maritza Jensen, Tiffany DeSantis, Ruth Welsch, Sara Gray, Sara Pearson, Shelly Swan, Valerie Waagen, Melissa Sorci, Janice O'Deegan, Andrea Lee, and Juana Olsen.

To my amazing parents, Heidi and Al Krautter who instilled in me a strong work ethic. You always supported me and taught me to give back to the community. This book is a way for me to do that. To my brother, Torsten Krautter, and his wife, Kim, your love and support means a lot to me.

To my incredible husband, Jason, whose constant encouragement and reassurance during the development of this book was invaluable. To my two amazing sons, Tyler and Brody, who had to give up several hours of "mommy time" in order to allow for the completion of this book.

To my incredible pre-teen and teenage patients who have been consistently open and honest with me about their experiences with their eating disorder. You are the source of my inspiration for writing this book. The readers ultimately have you to thank for their acquired information and knowledge. Thank you for sharing your journey of treatment and recovery with me and with them.

Thank you all!!

CONTENTS

INTRODUCTION

There is no denying that society evolves on a continual basis throughout time. I think most people would agree that this is not necessarily a bad thing. In fact, many changes are viewed as highly positive. However, this is not the case for all shifts in our society. It is for this reason that I have created a book series entitled *What Every Parent Needs to Know About ... .* that addresses a variety of topics. The sole purpose of this series is to educate parents about dangerous trends and behaviors that have become increasingly common among youth in our country. Some of these trends have evolved gradually over the past few decades. Others are startling new phenomena. In either case, they are present in our society today, and our children are likely to confront them.

This book, *What Every Parent Needs to Know About Eating Disorders,* focuses on the persistent trend of disordered eating. Unhealthy eating and negative perceptions of body image among our youth are pronounced. Simply stated, these two symptoms, in combination with a desire for perfection and a need for control, are often pre-cursors to the development of an eating disorder. In America, it is estimated that one out of every 200 females suffers from Anorexia Nervosa (AN), and two out of 100 females suffer from Bulimia Nervosa (BN). An estimated 10-15% of people with anorexia or bulimia are males. Our country faces an additional eating disorder, compulsive overeating, which leads to obesity. Although compulsive overeating is a highly significant problem in the United States, it is, unfortunately, beyond the parameters of this book.

National statistics on anorexia and bulimia reveal that the number of cases is increasing each year. Unfortunately, these statistics may not be fully accurate. Because of the secretiveness and shame associated with this problem, it is likely that many cases are uncounted. This is probably more true regarding males than females, since eating disorders are often considered to be a "female" problem. Throughout the book, when referencing an individual with an eating disorder, I will use female pronouns. This is not to say that males do not struggle with these illness; they do. It is simply for convenience, as it is representative of the majority of sufferers. It is not intended to offend readers who have a son struggling with an eating disorder.

What Every Parent Needs to Know About Eating Disorders describes the psychological and medical challenges faced by individuals trying to recover from an eating disorder. It provides education and understanding for parents who are interested in learning more about this potentially lethal behavior. By blending clinical expertise with personal stories, the book offers guidance and practical strategies that can be utilized by caregivers trying to help individuals suffering from this problem.

What Every Parent Needs to Know About Eating Disorders will educate the reader on all facets of anorexia nervosa and bulimia nervosa including cause and effect, cultural forces, risk assessment, treatment planning, therapeutic fit, relapse, and relapse prevention. In addition, the book will present a thorough understanding of both the physical and emotional consequences of eating disorders and how they affect the person socially, emotionally, educationally, and/or occupationally.

By exploring the roller-coaster of emotions that coincide with these conditions, parents will gain a better understanding of which responses are helpful, and which are more likely to be detrimental in dealing with a child suffering from an eating disorder. Armed with these tools and insights, parents will be better equipped to help their children through recovery. Ultimately, with proper understanding, support, and treatment, individuals can overcome an eating disorder.

****

I was inspired to write this book for three primary reasons. First, eating disorders are still largely misunderstood, even though they affect thousands of families. I feel compelled to emphasize that eating disorders do not only affect the individual sufferer but the family as a whole. As you will see through the many illustrations presented in this book, parents and siblings struggle significantly when their loved ones face these illnesses. It is for this reason that I strongly encourage family involvement in the treatment and recovery process. Family members are the greatest resource for the individual with these problems since the illness will be encountered on a daily basis at home.

The second source of inspiration for this book came from something I learned in my profession: Highly stressed individuals need a means to relieve their internal tension. This certainly applies to individuals with eating disorders. Some individuals deal with their distress in positive, healthy ways such as exercise, journaling, and/or artistic outlets. Others turn to negative and unhealthy means of stress relief, including substance abuse, self harm and/or disordered eating. For an individual with an eating disorder, it is usually a combination of this personal distress, along with certain personality traits, family dynamics, and cultural influences, that leads to the onset and maintenance of this illness.

Once fully established, the illness can be viewed as a cycle of negativity that has destructive consequences for the individual, and in turn, for everyone else in the family unit. Mental health professionals search constantly for creative ways to reduce a patient's isolation and help them to gain the support necessary to feel more understood. The opportunity to hear, and learn from the stories of other individuals who have dealt with eating disorders helps both patients and their families gain insight and feel less alone.

The third, and most important reason for writing this book, is to offer some tangible explanations and relief to parents confronted with a child who has an eating disorder. Parents typically feel hopeless and helpless when their child has been diagnosed with this illness. Perhaps this is mostly due to the fact that most kids who are diagnosed do not want to get help – at least not initially. This leaves the parents feeling like they are constantly fighting to keep their child alive without their child's cooperation. This can be infuriating for parents who simply do not understand what is so hard about something as basic as eating.

In this book, I offer a psychological perspective on both AN and BN and discuss how parents can cope with their child's illness. I also discuss the consequences of having an eating disorder present in the home, and review ways in which family members can help. In addition, I share many personal stories from individuals who went through treatment and recovery. I know that there are millions of people who have traveled the same path as families I reference in this book, and there will be millions more to come. I hope that the depiction of the mystifying and relentless world of eating disorders might somehow provide hope and solace to them.

In closing, I want to acknowledge that every child and family situation is different. I would never suggest that this book unlocks all the mysteries and manifestations of a child with an eating disorder. As readers will discover, eating disorders do frequently break the spirit of many individuals and their families for a period during treatment and recovery. For a while, many of the individuals presented in this book lost nearly all of the daily battles that recovery presented. On the other hand, they did manage to win the long term battle through perseverance, family support, and the timely discovery of substantive information along the way. It is my sincere hope that *What Every Parent Needs to Know About Eating Disorders* will increase the knowledge base of this illness while emboldening parents to believe that they, too, can survive their child's journey of recovery.

1

ANOREXIA NERVOSA

Sara is a 16 -year-old girl. Joey is a 17-year-old boy. Best friends since kindergarten, they do everything together. So it was no surprise to their parents when they went on the same diet in an attempt to lose ten pounds each. Sara wanted to lose weight for the winter ball and Joey needed to slim down for wrestling. They knew that motivating each other would help them both accomplish their goal. But what neither the teenagers nor their parents expected was that "a simple diet" would turn into a horrific illness that would almost take both their lives. Sara lost 40 pounds in four months. Over the course of one year, she was in and out of the hospital eight times. Joey lost 25 pounds in three months and suffered from fainting spells, severe dehydration, and a heart attack that nearly killed him. Neither teen had set out to lose that much weight. They both reported that "things spun out of control" and "it just happened."

WHAT IS ANOREXIA NERVOSA?

Anorexia Nervosa (AN) is a serious psychiatric illness characterized by persistent weight loss, distorted body image, and an intense fear of gaining weight. For females, an additional characteristic is amenorrhea, or loss of the menstrual cycle for at least three consecutive months. As indicated in the story above, AN is not only "a female disorder" as was once believed. However, it is still more common in females, with young women between the ages of 15 and 24 at the highest risk for acquiring the illness. According to the National Association of Anorexia Nervosa and Associated Disorders, AN is currently estimated to occur in up to 5% of all teenage girls in the United States of America and is listed as the third most common chronic illness in adolescent females. Seven million females and one million males suffer from eating disorders in our country.

Most people are unaware that there are two different types of AN: restricting and binge-eating/purging. Restricting AN is the most common, and is exactly what it sounds like: the person restricts their caloric intake leading to significant weight loss and malnutrition. The binge-eating/purging type of AN, although less common, occurs with surprising frequency throughout the course of the illness. This type of AN should not be confused with Bulimia Nervosa (BN). While BN will be more fully discussed in the next chapter, the main difference between AN, binge-eating/purging type, and BN, is the size of the binge. With AN, the binge is either an average size meal or more commonly, a very small amount of food. The person with AN distorts the amount of food consumed, becomes frightened that they ate too much, and engages in purging behavior. Since the binge is usually very small and then purged from the body, individuals with this type of AN also experience significant weight loss and malnutrition. By comparison, a typical bulimic binge is much larger.

Whether the individual suffers from restricting AN or binge-eating/purging AN, it is important to fully grasp the dangers of this eating disorder. AN has the highest mortality rate of all psychiatric disorders. This means that more people die from AN than from any other type of psychiatric illness – including alcohol and drug addiction, and depression. Approximately half of the deaths from AN are due to the medical consequences of the disease. The other half are due to suicide. This fact illustrates a very important concept in understanding AN. AN is both a mind and body disorder. This dual focus makes it twice as dangerous for sufferers because they are likely to experience both medical and psychological consequences as a result of the disease.

MEDICAL CONSEQUENCES OF ANOREXIA NERVOSA

Mild to severe medical complications can emerge as a result of AN, some of which are irreversible. The most common health problem is malnutrition which affects the circulatory, reproductive, and digestive systems of the body. While malnutrition affects all the muscles in the body, the most important muscle affected is the heart. In response to the lack of nutrients, the heart conserves energy by slowing down. This results in an irregular heartbeat. This condition can cause reduced blood flow in the body and a drop in blood pressure. If the heart slows too much, it may eventually stop, causing congestive heart failure or cardiac arrest. This outcome is very common with AN patients.

Hypothermia, or lower-than-normal body temperature, is another potential medical consequence. The drop in body temperature means the person often feels cold. This is why it is not uncommon to see an individual with AN wearing layers of clothing. It is not only a way for the individual to hide their significant weight loss from others, as most people would think, but also a way to keep warm. Interestingly, the body also finds ways to preserve warmth. To compensate for the drop in temperature, the body grows additional hair called lanugo. Lanugo is fine, downy hair that looks like feathers on a bird. It is the same hair that is on a fetus in utero to maintain body heat. It is usually most noticeable on the person's face and on the back of the neck, but is also often seen on the forearms and the back of the legs.

As the person with AN grows hair on her body, she often loses the hair on her head. Malnutrition causes the hair to become dry and brittle, and then to fall out. It is not uncommon for an individual with AN to be washing her hair in the shower and end up with a fistful of hair in her hand. This can be frightening and traumatic, as the patient usually do not understand the cause of this hair loss. She also often does not understand why there is a change in her skin texture and tone. Self-starvation makes the skin flaky, dry and pale. Sunken eyes and cheeks are often noticeable as well.

Bone density is affected when the female with AN becomes amenorrheic. As mentioned earlier, the lack of nutrition causes girls with AN to stop menstruating. When a female menstruates, certain hormones are released that allow calcium to be deposited into bones. If menstruation stops, calcium depletion follows, making the bones porous and susceptible to fractures and breaks. If the condition continues, long term effects include increased risk of osteoporosis. According to medical professionals, osteoporosis, which can be caused by malnutrition, and decreased estrogen secretion, can lead to growth retardation and decreased bone density.

Lastly, AN affects the digestive system. Metabolism slows to conserve food and energy and the digestive process is often disrupted, resulting in severe bloating and constipation. It is not uncommon for an individual to complain about feeling full when she has not eaten much food. This abdominal discomfort is commonly due to a delay in gastric emptying and it contributes significantly to the sufferer's resistance to treatment intervention and recovery.

If the individual with AN is practicing binge/purge behaviors, there are additional medical symptoms and consequences. These include   (1) enlarged salivary glands, (2) erosion of dental enamel, (3) calluses or skin abrasions on the hand caused by teeth from repeated induced vomiting, (4) chronic dehydration, and (5) electrolyte imbalances. The depletion of potassium is particularly serious and can lead to hypokalemia, which increases the risk of heart arrhythmia and kidney failure.   Medical professionals agree however, that with recovery, these consequences can be reversed.   These medical consequences underscore the strong need for a thorough medical assessment as part of the treatment for adolescents with AN.

PSYCHOLOGICAL CONSEQUENCES

There are multiple psychological consequences of AN, some of which are as severe and devastating as the medical consequences. Remember that half of the deaths attributable to AN are from medical consequences and the other half are due to suicide. When a person is malnourished, the entire body is affected, including the brain. A malnourished brain cannot function at its optimal level. The result is a range of psychological signs and symptoms that cause the person great distress.

Psychological   consequences   include   depression, anxiety, obsessions and compulsions, and thought disturbances. Often the person experiences a combination of all of these as she progresses more deeply into her eating disorder. However, it does not usually start out that way. In the beginning, there may be only a single symptom, such as poor concentration. The student, who has always focused well in school, is suddenly easily distracted and mentally fatigued. The teenager, who never gave much thought to what or how much she ate, begins to obsess about food, calories and body image. These thoughts can very quickly lead to depression and anxiety as well as obsessions and compulsions.

As mentioned earlier, in order to be clinically diagnosed with AN, individuals need to report distorted body image or deny the seriousness of their current low body weight. They place undue influence on body weight or shape in their self-evaluation and almost always perceive themselves as being much heavier than they actually are. This distorted perception leads to a fear of gaining weight that is so intense that restriction of food or purging behavior becomes inexorable.

When describing distorted body image to parents or mental health workers, I often use the example of looking into a fun house mirror. Those mirrors change the way your body looks, reflecting back an unrealistic and distorted image. This is what happens to an individual with AN. She may be skeletally thin; however, when she looks at herself, she sees a person who is overweight or even obese. This distortion may involve one specific body part or the entire body. In either case, the disparity is very upsetting to the individual - even though she is being told that she is very thin, she sees herself as fat.

I believe that having a distorted body image is the cruelest part of this illness. I also believe that it is also the most difficult part of the illness to recover from. If individuals with AN could see themselves the way that they really look, I believe they would engage more readily in treatment and enter recovery sooner. However, they do not see what others see, and at the same time, they know that they are not "crazy." So it is very hard for them to wrap their heads around the idea that their perception is distorted. Despite what others say, they believe that what they see is real, and that everyone else must be mistaken.

Unfortunately, this is the easier belief system to adopt. Especially since the person with AN is intensely afraid of gaining weight. If she admits to herself or others that she is underweight (which again she does not visibly observe), then she will have to enter treatment. Treatment for the individual with AN is very scary. Most people with this illness view getting help as getting fat. They believe that if they enter treatment, they will be forced to eat and gain weight. This obviously represents a huge conflict for them. They already see themselves as fat, so why in the world would they want to eat more and gain more weight? Consequently, they will avoid and resist treatment intervention. Moreover, even after weight restoration in treatment, body distortion may remain. Therefore, it is essential to reinforce to the individual with AN that getting better does not mean "getting fat." It means (at least in part) no longer seeing themselves in a distorted way.

Another reason why recovering from a distorted self-perception is so hard is that individuals with AN are often consumed with irrational and unproductive thoughts regarding food, calories, and weight. These thoughts are often referred to as "Anorexic Thoughts" or "Eating Disorder Thoughts." They are usually highly illogical and cause the person great psychological distress especially since they consume a large percentage of the person's thoughts in a day.

I often ask my patients with AN how often they think about food, weight, calories, and body image. Without exception, the response is 90% of the time or more. Most are consumed by these thoughts constantly, which is highly anxiety-provoking and depressing. Imagine spending 90% – 100% of your day ruminating about how bad you look and how you need to avoid food and the impulse to eat.

Eventually, these obsessive thoughts take over the patient's life. The individual with AN becomes isolated from friends and family, moody, and short-tempered. To better understand this, think about how it feels to miss a meal. Most people become irritable. This is what happens to people with AN in an exaggerated way because they have been missing meals for months. Parents of AN sufferers often complain that their child is always angry and unhappy. One parent related a story in which she simply asked her daughter what she wanted to do on a Saturday afternoon. In response, the daughter screamed at the mother to leave her alone, then slammed to door to her room. This type of behavior was not present before the daughter developed her eating disorder.   Another story is from a teacher, who watched her best student became constantly irritable and distracted in class. When asked to answer a question on an oral quiz, the student grunted and said, "That is a stupid question, but I'll answer it anyway."

Since the person with AN will never see herself as thin (remember she must have distorted body image to be diagnosed with this illness), there is no relief from her negative thoughts while she is struggling with this disorder. In other words, as long as she has this illness, she will always see herself as overweight or obese. Most individuals who have struggled with this illness for a long period of time eventually become tired of continuously feeling bad. This is often when they become suicidal. They are exhausted by the constant anxiety, and feelings of hopelessness and depression. Death starts to look like a welcome release.

CAUSES OF ANOREXIA NERVOSA

There are many hypotheses about the cause of AN. There is a growing consensus among professionals that there is probably not a single basis for the development of this disorder, but rather a combination of factors that contribute to the onset of the illness.   Family and cultural influences, genetic, biological, and medical factors, psychological characteristics, and infections have all been identified as possible causes and contributors to the onset and maintenance of AN.

Because there is widespread uncertainty about the underlying cause or causes, AN is considered particularly difficult to treat. The treatment is complicated and often long-term. Mental health professionals recognize the need for a successful treatment plan since self-starvation has become a growing epidemic in Western society. Unfortunately, to date no treatment has been recognized unequivocally as being highly effective in the treatment of this illness.

WHAT PLACES MY CHILD AT RISK: CHARACTERISTICS ASSOCIATED WITH AN

Parents often ask me whether their child is likely to develop an eating disorder. This is difficult to answer because there are multiple factors that may place a person at risk. Many adolescents with AN share feelings of being out of control, of wanting to return to a younger, less stressful time in their lives, and of perceiving their own maturing body as foreign and unwanted. Cognition patterns associated with eating disorders include a tendency toward dichotomous (all or nothing) thinking, low self-esteem and fear of intimacy. Finally, researchers have identified several personality traits that are common among AN sufferers, including perfectionism and a high drive to achieve.

CONTROL

Many of my patients with AN refer to a need for control. Individuals who perceive a lack of control over themselves and their environment often compensate by attempting to gain control in other areas of their life. One

of the easiest areas to achieve control involves the body –
specifically, what goes into or out of it. This isolated area
of personal control can become obsessive and lead to an
eating disorder if not monitored.

Adolescents often start to feel out of control as they
encounter greater demands and responsibility in their
lives at school (i.e., more homework, tests, etc.), at home
(i.e., chores), at work (i.e., tasks in an after school job),
and/or in extracurricular activities (i.e., more competition
in sports, music, art, etc.). This often leads to fantasies of
easier times, when there was less responsibility, less inde-
pendence, and fewer demands.

AN can be seen as the ultimate regression. Physical
appearance, bodily processes, emotions, and cognitions all
change with the onset and maintenance of this illness.
Physically, the individual with AN loses a substantial
amount of weight. As body size decreases, the person
appears smaller and much younger looking than her actual
age. In addition, let's not forget that if the person with AN
is female, she will also stop menstruating, which brings her
back to pre-pubescent times. The change in physical
appearance, along with becoming amenorrheic, provides
females with a way to remain in a child's body, thus
avoiding the responsibilities and demands of adulthood.

PERCEPTION OF THE BODY AS FOREIGN

Many kids are not taught that their bodies will change
constantly through puberty and beyond. Certainly they
learn the basics in health class and/or from their parents
about puberty, but often they do not fully understand that

this is a process that does not take place overnight and does not stop at a certain age. In actuality, the body changes throughout a lifetime. Without this education, many adolescents and adults alike feel as though their bodies are foreign to them because they are not doing what they would like them to do, or are changing in ways that they did not "sign up for."

Take for example, the girl who knew all about puberty and the physical changes her body would undergo at age 11, but then in young adulthood, did not understand why her body was still changing. She called it "thickening out." This may have happened to her in part from what some call the "Freshman 15" – less healthy eating and a few too many fraternity parties, but also because the body changes with almost every decade. Metabolism and a change in hormones all play a part in this. This is true for both boys and girls. A lack of education about these changes places the adolescent at great risk for developing AN, as the body becomes a source of discomfort.

Several experts in the field agree that the perception of the body as being foreign or unnatural makes it easier for the individual with AN to control it in an artificial way through food restriction or binge eating and purging. A study conducted by Attie and Brooks-Gunn (1989) tested the hypothesis that the development of eating problems represents an accommodation to puberty. They found that eating problems developed during puberty, particularly in response to fat accumulation. The study followed 7th to 10th grade girls for a period of two years. The girls who reported negative body images while going through puberty were at the highest risk for eating problems.

"ALL OR NOTHING" THINKING & LOW SELF ESTEEM

The way the adolescent with AN feels, and the way she thinks seem to go hand-in-hand. Individuals with AN characteristically have a particular thinking style. Their cognitions are focused on extremes, which is often referred to as the "all or nothing" thinking style. A dichotomous thinking style places the adolescent at high risk for low self-esteem. Since there is no gray area within the dichotomy, the adolescent sees herself as either all good or all bad. Her self-esteem is highly dependent on external forces.

Family, culture, and peer groups are all very influential in the lives of adolescents with AN, causing them to be highly vulnerable when around these subsystems. The motivation to be successful comes from the need to please others, not from within. These influences and motivations are indicative of earlier phases of development. According to Mahler's developmental theory (1975), an individual with low self-esteem will have greater difficulty achieving the developmental task of separation and individuation and remain in an earlier phase of development.

SEX/SEXUAL ABUSE

As mentioned earlier, the desire to avoid the demands and responsibilities of adulthood is a potential cause for the development of an eating disorder. These responsibilities might include becoming intimate with others and engaging in sexual behaviors. The possibility of intimacy is particularly scary for an adolescent who has a history of sexual abuse. In this case, AN may protect the adolescent from the fears of intimacy by shifting the focus from the past abuse to a preoccupation with food and weight.

Researchers have theorized that individuals who have been sexually abused feel a sense of loss. This loss is a loss of control over what was done to them. During the trauma, the person has no control over their body or over their perpetrator's body. This lack of control is highly distressing. It is not uncommon for abuse victims to try to regain control, and one way they may attempt to do it is by engaging in the restriction of food or in the binge-purge cycle. This is not to say that all adolescents diagnosed with AN have been sexually abused, nor is it so say that sexual abuse causes AN, but the correlation between sexual abuse and AN is significant.

PERFECTIONISM & DRIVE TO ACHIEVE

Perfectionism and drive are two personality traits that are often associated with individuals diagnosed with AN. These two characteristics are seen much more commonly among adolescents who restrict food intake versus adolescents who binge eat and purge. The individual who restricts food is much more rigid and driven to achieve her perception of the perfect body weight and shape. Many researchers believe that adolescents who achieve weight loss have a sense of accomplishment. This sense of achievement then leads to further weight loss which often can precipitate, or contribute to the maintenance of, AN. For example, Fairburn et al. (1999) believe that the individual's attempts at perfectionism and weight control provide her with a sense of accomplishment and self-worth when faced with deep feelings of ineffectiveness in society.

For the individual with AN, the drive to be perfect is not only observed in relation to body image. Frequently, observations can be made in many different settings. For example, it is common for individuals diagnosed with AN to have a strong desire for perfectionism at school either in the classroom or in extra-curricular activities such as sports. These characteristics can also be seen in a work setting and at home.

Unfortunately, these personality traits can affect the relationships they have with others. Many of my patients have stated that their drive to be perfect was so strong that it caused them to stay away from others. They said that they often ignored everything and everyone else around them. Socially isolating themselves led to conflictual and/or strained relationships with family, friends, and teachers. One of my teens noted, "I went from being charismatic, energetic, and sympathetic" to "avoidant, suspicious, and introverted." It is common for an individual struggling with AN to experience a detachment from her feelings, an inability to trust, and impaired social skills.

Overall, a review of the literature on the personality characteristics of an adolescent with AN results in inconsistent findings. However, a general profile was identified for the adolescent with AN, restricting type, in a doctoral research paper written by Cynthia Regardie (1994).

Regardie described this adolescent as a chronically imma-
ture, socially isolated, passive-aggressive individual who
exhibits signs and symptoms of depression, anxiety, and
thought disturbance (such as distorted body image). The
profile also included descriptions of being obsessional,
having low ego strength, and having a limited awareness of
psychological problems.

TREATING ANOREXIA NERVOSA

I will discuss in great detail the overall treatment of
both AN and BN later in this book. However, I would like
to briefly address some specifics on the treatment of AN
here. AN is a pernicious illness that should be treated
aggressively from the start. Follow your instincts as a
parent. If you think your child is in trouble, seek professional consultation. Do not assume that your child is
going through a phase, or that significant weight loss in a
relatively short period of time simply represents willpower
and a good diet. If your child is in trouble, he or she needs
your quick response. I cannot tell you how many parents
come to my office for an initial consultation only to find
that, after I refer them to a medical doctor, their child is
immediately sent to the hospital because their vital signs
are unstable. The surprise comes from the fact that you
cannot visibly see problems with blood pressure, heart
rate or temperature. Accordingly, prompt medical assistance to assess the severity of the problem is imperative.

For Joey's parents, it was not until he started fainting at
his wrestling matches that they developed major concerns. Sara's parents could tell more quickly that she had a

problem because they could see her body drastically shrinking in size. It is my firm opinion that parents are the greatest advocates for their children. Don't be afraid to talk to your children about your concerns and get them the support they need.

I have had several parents share with me that they were certain their child had a problem, but when they took their child to the pediatrician, the pediatrician reported being unconcerned at the time. This lack of concern might be due to the fact that the child's vital signs were normal, or a belief that the child was in the middle of a growth spurt. In either case, do not be afraid to ask for a follow-up appointment sooner rather than later. Just because your child is medically stable at one appointment does not mean that she will be medically stable at the next one – even just a few weeks later. Everyone's body is different. When a person has AN, her body often functions for a while on physical reserves. When these reserves run out, the decline into medical instability may be precipitous.

For example, after several months of self-starvation, Sarah was severely underweight (83% of her ideal body weight). It was at this time that her parents first got her in to see a doctor. The doctor told them that she was medically stable. In fact, she was medically stable even when she went down to 78% of her ideal body weight. The doctors could not figure out why, at this weight, her vital signs were normal. The day after her vital signs were checked by her pediatrician, she fainted and ended up in the hospital for medical instability. This was her first hospitalization, with many more to follow due to the trauma she caused her body. Sarah's parents strongly believed that she needed to be hospitalized much earlier than when she became medically unstable. Unfortunately, hospitals will not often accept patients who are medically stable even though they are severely underweight. This is changing with the risk of medical instability, but it is variable from hospital to hospital and insurance company to insurance company.

The good news is that there is hope. Individuals can and do recover from this illness with the proper medical and mental health care. Psychotherapy is considered vital in progressing toward recovery and should be sought as soon as possible. For more information and specifics about treatment, see chapter 5.

2

BULIMIA NERVOSA

TARYN'S STORY

For as long as Taryn could remember, she was always self-conscious about her weight. Although one could argue that almost every female in Western society is self-conscious about her weight at some point in her life, when a woman is struggling with an eating disorder, this discomfort is heightened drastically. Taryn first developed what she would formally call an "eating disorder" when she was in high school. Now, over a decade later, she can finally say she is fully recovered.

Taryn is 5'6" tall, and back then weighed what she thought was a disgusting 138 pounds. She had tried diets and exercise in the past, but they would only last a few weeks before she gave up. She had tried using her mom's diet pill, but those did not work either. Teenage life was hard and being "fat" made it even harder. She graduated from high school wanting to be happy, but feeling miserable. She constantly compared herself to her friends who all looked incredibly thin and beautiful. She wondered why her legs looked so large and her hips so wide when everyone else seemed to have the perfect body.

Taryn decided to do something about her weight before entering college. She started to count calories, exercise daily and cut fat from her diet. Eventually, she began skipping meals, and then stopped eating altogether on most days. If she ate even the smallest amount of food, she felt guilty and called herself a failure. She doubled her exercise routine after consuming liquid to get rid of the water weight. She chewed gum instead of food. She stayed away from any social gatherings in which food was present, which meant most of them.

All of these methods worked for a while, but eventually Taryn could not keep up the regimen. She found herself craving high calorie foods and eventually binging on them. One time she binged so much, she felt sick. Taryn panicked. She was petrified of gaining weight and furious with herself for putting herself in this situation.   She needed to get the food out of her and fast. Taryn knew what Bulimia was, and even though she had heard terrible stories about girls with eating disorders, she wanted to see if it would work.

No one was home the day she decided to try it. She went into the bathroom, stuck her finger down her throat, and made herself throw up. Taryn thought she would feel terrible or disgusting or even guilty, but instead she felt great. She walked out of the bathroom with a huge smile on her face, feeling as if she had conquered the world. Later she would say, "The problem is that things can get really serious when something you think is totally under your control turns into an obsession." Vomiting quickly became Taryn's guiltless way to eat whatever she wanted with little fear of weight gain. Pretty soon it was all she ever did and all she ever thought about. She stopped inviting friends over to her house. Bulimia became her best friend. She didn't care about anyone but herself and her eating disorder. She binged and purged up to five times a day for more than five years before seeking treatment.

Her family and friends encouraged treatment much earlier, but as a legal adult, treatment could not be forced. Taryn was unwilling to see someone. She was not ready to give up her illness. She tried to convince others that she was fine; that they were mistaken about her. She gave reasons for her incessant baking, then snuck the food up to her room where she could eat it all by herself. She would devour a batch of brownies that she had so beautifully wrapped as a "gift" for a friend, or finish off an entire bowl of cookie dough in one night. She told people that she was devastated that the five course meal she had been cooking all day got ruined and ended up in the garbage instead of in her stomach. She snuck out to fast food restaurants and ate in the car before going home. Her behavior became so out of control that she would eat anything she could get her hands on in larger and larger amounts. Her body became so accustomed to consuming large amounts of food and then quickly purging it that whenever she bent over she would automatically throw up. She didn't even have to stick her finger down her throat anymore.

Things came to a head one day when Taryn noticed that she threw up blood. She was not exactly sure what this meant at the time, but she did know that this was a serious problem. She decided to reach out to her roommate and tell her about her problem with bulimia. Her roommate took her to the emergency room and Taryn was admitted for tests. A thorough evaluation of her physical and mental health took place. It was during this time that Taryn began to take stock of all the scary effects of this illness on her well-being. She had stopped menstruating for ten consecutive months, her skin was so dry it actually hurt, and all the color had left her face. Her hair had started to fall out of her head and she had grown hair on her arms and legs as a way to compensate for the fat loss on her body. She was cold all the time and constantly exhausted. When exercising, she felt as if she was going to pass out and had fainted on more than ten occasions (once acquiring a laceration on her forehead that required stitches and a creative story about tripping and falling when jogging on a park trail). She lost friends and close family ties. She became much more isolated and egocentric. She stopped participating in things that she once found interesting, desirable and pleasurable. All that mattered to her were her binges and purges.

Luckily, Taryn got the help she needed. She sought out a team of eating disorder specialists and began treatment and recovery immediately. She realized that she needed to treat this serious illness aggressively. She met weekly with a therapist for both individual and group counseling; she met monthly with a nutritionist for meal planning; and she met bi-monthly with a medical doctor to ensure medical stability. In treatment, Taryn explored the reasons why she began engaging in this behavior and why she had maintained this negative coping mechanism for close to a decade. With the help of her team, she began utilizing alternative behaviors to help her meet her needs in a healthier and more functional way. Taryn's story is one of desperation, hope, and success.

WHAT IS BULIMIA NERVOSA?

Bulimia Nervosa (BN) is a serious psychiatric illness. This eating disorder is characterized by persistent binge eating (usually starches and sweets) and then inappropriate weight control. The most common type of inappropriate weight control is vomiting or the use of laxatives and/or diuretics. However, other types of inappropriate measures are taken by individuals who suffer from bulimia as well. For example, the person may restrict their food by fasting for several days after a binge. They might also exercise excessively in order to compensate for the high amount of calories they have ingested. In either case, bulimia (purging type or non-purging type) should be considered a serious illness and treated aggressively as quickly as possible.

WHAT IS A BINGE?

Many people wonder what constitutes a binge. Parents come into my office all the time asking if their child has a problem because they see large quantities of food eaten and no indications of weight gain. Is this a growth spurt? Is their child not eating at other times of the day? Or are they struggling with an eating disorder that warrants intervention? If your child is binging on food, two things will be true. First, she/he consumes much more food than most people would in a similar circumstance and in a similar period of time. In other words, eating large quantities of food during Thanksgiving dinner would not necessarily be considered a bulimic binge. However, eating an entire box of cereal, a large pizza, or finishing off an entire birthday cake by oneself in a short period of time on a random Monday afternoon after school would constitute a binge.

In addition, when the person is engaged in the binging behavior, they feel very much out of control. My patients often say things like "I couldn't stop myself," or "It was as if I was driven by a motor." This is perhaps one of the most distressing parts of this illness; the feeling of being out of control. Imagine a teenager who leaves school and goes to McDonald's and orders a meal deal, then stops by an ice cream shop and gets a double sundae. Next they go home, and if their stomach is not completely full yet (it expands with the large quantities that are taken in), they find something else to consume. Due to physical discomfort, fear, or even disgust, the person then rids themselves of the food - usually by purging.

DIAGNOSING BULIMIA

In order to be formally diagnosed with bulimia, both of the behaviors mentioned above (binge eating and inappropriate weight control) have to occur at least twice a month for at least three consecutive months. For many this is the case. However, for others it is not. As a warning, I tell parents that if their child is engaging in these behaviors even on an irregular basis, act fast to get her into treatment. Bulimia can be extremely habit-forming. There is some research that shows it is addictive. During the purging process the body is highly stimulated, followed by a sense of calm when the purging is complete. Patients have compared this feeling to intense exercise, sexual intercourse, and other addictive behaviors. It is common for infrequent bouts with binging and purging to quickly become much more frequent. Several of my patients have stated that within a few months they went from irregular, inconsistent bulimic behavior, to binging and purging several times a day.

Bulimia does not have as high of a mortality rate as does AN. Approximately 2% of sufferers die from bulimia. The person with bulimia is usually of average weight or a little bit above. This makes it much harder for parents and health practitioners to detect, since the person is not malnourished.

The overall incidence of bulimia is increasing. There is evidence that the disorder is increasing in females between the ages of 13 and 18. According to the National Association of Anorexia Nervosa and Associated Disorders (ANAD, 2000), bulimia is currently estimated to occur in up to 1-2% of all teenage girls in the United States of America, and is listed as the fourth most common chronic illness in adolescent females.

MEDICAL CONSEQUENCES OF BULIMIA

There are several medical consequences associated with bulimia. Unfortunately, the repetitive act of binging and purging affects many of the systems in the body. The most dangerous effect is on the muscles in the body, and specifically the heart. Electrolyte imbalance is a common problem for individuals with bulimia. Low potassium levels are particularly dangerous and could cause heart failure. Binging and purging as well as binging and restricting behaviors affect the digestive system. As with sufferers of AN, metabolism is slowed to conserve food and energy and the digestive process is often disrupted, resulting in severe bloating and constipation.

An individual who engages in purging behaviors may cause ruptures or tears in their stomach and/or esophagus as well as intestinal damage through the use of laxatives. In addition, the purging causes tooth decay as the stomach acid erodes the enamel on the teeth as it comes up with the food. Dentists are often the first medical practitioners to alert parents of this problem from their visual observations.

PSYCHOLOGICAL CONSEQUENCES

There are multiple psychological consequences of BN that can cause the person great distress. Many of these consequences are similar to those experienced by individuals diagnosed with AN. The individual may experience depression, anxiety, impulse control problems, and thought disturbances. Often the person experiences a combination of all of these as they progress more deeply into their eating disorder. However, like AN, it does not usually start out that way. In the beginning, there may be only a single symptom, such as irritability. The student, who has always been relaxed and happy, is suddenly angry and annoyed with others for no apparent reason. The teenager, who customarily would control her food intake by "watching what she ate," begins to lose control and eat whatever she wants in large quantities. These shifts in mood and behavior can quickly lead to depression and anxiety.

As mentioned in the previous chapter, individuals with AN are often consumed with irrational and unproductive thoughts regarding food, calories, and weight. Individuals with BN also become consumed with "Eating Disorder Thoughts." However, they do not tend to focus on calories and weight nearly as much, since part of their illness includes compensatory methods to deal with the ingestion of food. Instead, their thoughts focus predominantly on food, body image, and control or lack of control. These thoughts are usually highly illogical and cause the person great psychological distress especially since they occur with great frequency.

I often ask my patients with BN how often they think about food, body image, and control. The response tends to be 90% of the time or more. Most are consumed by these thoughts constantly, which is anxiety-provoking and depressing. Imagine spending 90% – 100% of your day ruminating about when you can binge without others finding out, what you can binge on, and how you will compensate for eating so much. In addition, sufferers of BN tend to beat themselves up constantly for having so little control over their binge eating. They often experience a high level of guilt and shame for engaging in this type of behavior. This is quite different from individuals who suffer from AN. Sufferers of AN feel proud of their accomplishment and ability to restrict food.

Eventually, the eating disorder thoughts take over the patient's life. The individual with BN becomes isolated from friends and family, moody, and short-tempered. With the AN patient, I asked you to think about how it feels to miss a meal. Most people become irritable. This is what happens to people with BN when they compensate for a binge by fasting for several days or weeks. Now think about how it feels when you have literally eaten so much that you feel sick. If this has never happened to you, think about a time when you got the stomach flu. What does vomiting do to your body? Not only does it cause you to feel weak and light-headed, but you may become dehydrated, experience a persistent sore throat from continual vomiting, and be left with the harsh taste of stomach acid in your mouth.

These effects, in and of themselves, would cause a person to be in a bad mood. Just imagine experiencing feelings of guilt, shame, embarrassment, and disgust on top of that. This is how individuals with BN feel every time they purge. Conversely, purging also makes them feel relieved, less fearful, and exhilarated. These feelings stem from the fact that they are determined to get rid of all the food they just ate. In part, they feel this way because they are physically uncomfortable. It does not feel good to stuff your stomach to its limits. Getting rid of the feeling of fullness is a positive sensation. In fact, it is probably one of the biggest motivators for purging. The majority of my patients have mixed feelings about purging.

Like parents of AN sufferers, parents of BN sufferers complain that their child is constantly angry and unhappy. One parent related a story in which she asked her daughter where she wanted to spend the holidays this year. In response, her daughter stood up and rudely said, "You are completely useless. You can't even make a stupid decision about where we should go for Christmas!" She then told her mother to "figure it out," and to leave her alone. The mother maintains that she never experienced this type of behavior prior to the onset of her daughter's eating disorder.

RECOGNIZING BULIMIA

Signs of bulimia often reported by parents, teachers, coaches, or friends include such behaviors as (1) immediate trips to the bathroom following meals; (2) the use of running water in the bathroom to hide the noise of vomiting; (3) constant sore throats, (4) cuts/teeth marks on the fore fingers as a result of biting as a gag reflex when the person sticks their finger down their throat to purge, (5) empty wrappers found in hiding places around the house to conceal binges; (6) discussion of weight and a focus on body image, (7) large quantities of food found missing that nobody in the house claims they ate or even saw, and (8) actual observation of binges, purging, fasting and/or excessive exercise.

CAUSES OF BULIMIA

There is no single cause of bulimia. In fact, it has been found that a combination of factors contribute to the onset of this illness such as psychological characteristics family influences, cultural influences, genetic, biological, and medical factors, and infections. Many patients with bulimia state that it is a physical way for them to handle chaos and a feeling of being overwhelmed in their lives. In addition, it is a way for them to take attention off something else in their lives that is highly distressing, such as a death of a parent, sibling illness, parental conflict or school failure. By engaging in these behaviors they literally fill themselves up and then purge away their distress. The binging behavior represents the chaotic (out of control) feelings they have in their life and the purging or non-purging methods give them this control back. It is no wonder that this cycle can become habit-forming.

TREATING BULIMIA

As mentioned in the last chapter on AN, I will focus on the treatment of eating disorders in great detail later in this book. However, I would briefly like to mention some specifics on the treatment of BN here. If you are unsure if there is a problem, simply let your child know that you will be seeking the services of an expert to help assess the severity of the situation. If your daughter had chest pains, you would take her to a cardiologist. If your son had cancer, you would have him seen by an oncologist. If you are not a doctor, don't claim to be one. Let your child know that all of her/his health care needs will be attended to because you care.

It is much harder for parents to recognize BN than AN. As a result, many children who suffer from this type of eating disorder are left untreated. Therefore, recognizing early warning signs is very important. As a parent it is important to know that if your child has an eating disorder, she has it for a reason. Having your child attend treatment sessions will allow her to find out what this reason is because often times they do no know themselves. I instruct parents NOT tell their child to stop the eating disorder behavior. This will only cause your child to be more secretive and less open about the problem. On the other hand, it would be completely inappropriate to encourage this behavior in any way. Eating disorders do fulfill some need for the individual, but the goal is to try to understand what that need is so that you can help your child learn to engage in alternative, healthy behaviors that will fulfill the same need. This work should be done in counseling sessions with a trained professional who can work with your child and with you as parents.

The greatest resource for a child with an eating disorder is often her parents. Don't minimize the amount of positive influence your family can have on the struggling family member. Help your child see that she is more than an eating disorder. Helping her understand and see that her identity is separate from bulimia is paramount. It is hard to fight against yourself; it is much easier to fight against a behavior. The good news is that eating disorders are treatable. The sooner the person enters treatment, the higher the success rates. For more information on treatment, see Chapter 5.

3

PREVENTION

EARLY DETECTION

One of the most effective ways to prevent the development of an eating disorder is to identify emerging symptoms early. As mentioned earlier, AN and BN are very aggressive illnesses. Therefore, they must be treated aggressively (which will be discussed in detail in the next two chapters). If parents and caregivers can recognize and respond quickly to symptoms, even though they may seem benign, there is a good possibility that these devastating disorders can be stopped before they start.

Early detection means that parents must be careful not to overlook, or minimize signs and symptoms of an eating disorder. While it seems ludicrous to suggest that a parent would minimize a potentially lethal problem, in my experience, it happens all the time. Parents do not do this because they are uncaring or neglectful. They do it because our society tells us that thin is good and thin is beautiful. Parents want their children to be happy and successful and to look good. Until parents are given some sort of indication that their child's health may be at risk, they are usually not alarmed and thus do not intervene.

Parents are not the only ones who may brush off symptoms. In my professional experience, coaches, teachers, and even doctors have all done this. A coach believes his star athlete is losing weight due to the level of training she is participating in, not the fact that she is exercising five hours a day while consuming only 500 calories per day. Coaches, like parents, want their kids (their athletes) to be successful. Sometimes weight loss helps them improve their chances for success. This might be true for long distance runners, gymnasts, ballet dancers, or wrestlers.

As mentioned previously, even pediatricians sometimes fail to recognize the early signs of an eating disorder, and may attribute sudden weight loss to a growth spurt. Since this is a plausible reason, many parents stop worrying. However, once the parents' concerns are assuaged, they often do not follow up with the doctor until it is too late. Doctors, like parents, quickly shift their opinion and move toward treatment when they recognize a continuous decline in weight and the onset of medical instability. Unfortunately, it is often too late to prevent the illness when this occurs, and we must move into the intervention stage.

ASSESSING YOUR CHILD

Parents often ask me how they can assess the situation with their child. While most parents are willing to have their children attend therapy sessions if there is not a diagnosed problem, some parents are uncomfortable bringing their child in to treatment without being certain that there is "something wrong." They prefer to shield their child from a visit with a counselor, and any associated stigma they may feel. Actually this presents parents with a wonderful opportunity to teach their children that going to see a therapist is one of the many ways people can explore any issues that may be of concern. It can be seen as similar as going to the pediatrician for a routine check-up.

Parents who are uncomfortable bringing their child to a therapist without a formal diagnosis in place may want to consider asking their child some of the questions listed below. While this list of questions can help open the lines of communication, it is important to remember that a parent should never try to be their child's therapist. Many kids are not comfortable answering their parents' questions about sensitive matters in the first place. They are often much more at ease talking to an objective person who has expertise in the area.

Accordingly, my first recommendation is always that parents ask their child whether they would prefer to speak with a professional, or with the parent. If the child prefers talking to a counselor, it usually means that they are worried about something going on in their lives, and the best thing to do is to set up an appointment for them. This answer also means that they are motivated to talk to someone, and when the child cooperates rather than resists, therapy is much more successful. Lastly, kids usually have great respect for their parents when they are allowed to make the choice in who they see. It is empowering for them, and often leads to greater investment in therapy.

PARENT ASSESSMENT QUESTIONS

Ask the following:

1. Do you think you restrict/binge/purge/over-exercise? If so, do you feel compulsively drawn to engage in this behavior?
2. Do you think you are below, average or overweight? What do you think of your body?
3. Does food, calories, or body image consume your thoughts or interfere with your ability to function normally? This includes socially, academically, and occupationally.
4. Realistically, could you stop the restricting/binging/purging/over-exercising today if you wanted to?

It is very important for parents to understand that if their child answers yes to any of these questions, they should immediately seek professional consultation and assessment. Remember that an individual has an eating disorder for a reason. A professional needs to work with your child to find out why.

Whether your child talks to you about signs and symptoms or whether you observe them yourself, it is important to remember that as a parent, you do NOT want to minimize the problem. You also do not want to tell your child to stop the behavior. Unfortunately, this does not work! If it was that simple, your child probably would stop the behavior, especially once she realized the damage it was doing to her physical and emotional well-being.

Eating disorders fulfill some need for the individual. If your child knows what that need is, and is willing to share this information with you, show your support by listening to what she has to say. Try to understand what her need is, and promote alternative behaviors that fulfill the same need in healthier ways (see appendix A). However, be careful not to permit the child to engage in other unhealthy behaviors. For example, if your child is binging and purging, do not encourage her to restrict or over-exercise.

When talking to your child, and trying to obtain information, be careful to avoid power struggles. Remember to keep your own emotions in check. If you find yourself getting angry, frustrated, blameful, or critical, walk away and resume the conversation at another time. These types of emotions are unproductive and can actually cause your child to shut down altogether. Trust your instincts. If you believe your child has a problem, but she is not willing to talk to you or admit that there is one, don't push it. Take some time to regroup and talk with her later.

If your child refuses to talk to you, make an appointment with an expert in the field. Experts are trained in interviewing techniques, and are skilled in getting kids to open up about their struggles. Remember that eating disorders make people sneaky, manipulative, and willing to lie. They do not see things clearly and will try anything to avoid intervention.

WARNING SIGNS

In earlier chapters, I talk about warning signs of both anorexia and bulimia. I would like to reiterate them in this chapter because actions often speak louder than words. If your child will not answer your questions and refuses to talk to you about your concerns, then you can make your own behavioral observations to determine if there is a problem. Below I have listed several observable warning signs that can indicate if your child may be in trouble.

WARNING SIGNS OF ANOREXIA NERVOSA:

1. Sudden weight loss
2. Distorted body image by subjective report
3. Constant complaints of being fat
4. Fear/avoidance of eating certain foods
5. Amenorrheic if female (stops getting periods)
6. Cutting out all or most fat from her diet
7. Suddenly wanting to be a vegetarian or vegan
8. Complaints of being cold all the time even in warm weather
9. Wearing layers of clothing (due to being cold and/or as a way to hide weight loss)
10. Pale skin
11. Sunken eyes
12. Hair loss on head
13. Hair growth on body (called lanugo, which looks like peach fuzz, to keep the body warm)

14. Difficulty concentrating
15. Lack of energy
16. Isolation from others
17. Avoidance of peers
18. Irritability
19. Mood lability
20. Complaints of being full when little or no food has been consumed

WARNING SIGNS OF BULIMIA

1. Visits to the bathroom after meals
2. Water running when in the bathroom to hide the sounds of purging
3. Continual complaints of a sore throat
4. Bite marks on the pointer and middle fingers where the teeth clench down during gag reflex
5. Laxatives and/or diuretics in the home
6. Tooth erosion
7. Smell of vomit on your child's breath or clothing
8. Food or blood found in the toilet
9. Large amounts of food missing from the house that nobody admits to having eaten
10. Large amounts of food eaten by your child with no sign of weight gain
11. Food hidden around the house in strange places
12. Wrappers found hidden in strange places
13. Consumption of large meals followed by excessive exercise or fasting

PREVENTION: THE IMPORTANCE OF ROLE MODELING

A large part of prevention involves knowing what may cause or trigger the onset of an eating disorder. Although some causes may not be avoidable, such as personality traits, infection, trauma, and family problems, other triggers can be investigated and prevented. One such trigger involves parental role modeling. Parents need to understand that it is their responsibility to model healthy eating and healthy body image for their children. This can be challenging for parents, especially if they have difficulty engaging in healthy eating themselves.

Kids observe adult behavior constantly, and look to us for guidance all the time. Notice I said they **LOOK** to us for guidance. Most kids don't ask for guidance from their parents or other adult role models in their lives unless they come from a family that is very communicative and open. However, just because they don't ask for guidance does not mean that they do not **OBSERVE** what the adults around them are doing. For example, I have had several kids tell me that their parent(s) are always on diets. Some of their parents lose weight and are ecstatic, and others fail at weight loss and are miserable. Whatever the outcome, the person's mood is highly affected. The individuals who have lost weight feel more confident and are elated by their new bodies. Those who have gained weight are depressed and feel hopeless. Kids are smart. It does not take a rocket scientist to recognize that their parents agree with society - thin is good, fat is bad.

If you are engaging in behaviors that illustrate disordered eating or a desperate attempt to lose weight, it is extremely likely that your child is aware of it. I cannot tell you how many kids have told me all the details of their parents' food habits. One of my patients tried to mimic her father, who ate only cabbage and rice for a month, in hope of losing weight as well as having something to discuss with him at the dinner table. Another one of my patients knew her mother's exact caloric intake when she was in training for a marathon.

Kids are computer savvy. Many of them hack into their parents' private computer files to find this information and learn more about them. They also hack past the parental controls on their own computers so they can visit any site on the Internet without their parents' knowledge (we will address this later). When it comes to eating disorders, many sites are not even prohibited by parental controls. For example, have you heard about the pro-eating disorder websites that are available to our youth online? These will be discussed in more detail below under the heading "The Dangers of Group Think." Knowing that all of this occurs is even more of a reason for parents to talk with their children about healthy eating and healthy body image.

SOCIETAL TRENDS THAT FOSTER EATING DISORDERS

As mentioned in previous chapters, society also plays a role in the development of an eating disorder. American society, more so than many other nationalities, has several defining features that support the development and maintenance of an eating disorder. I have created a list of these below. Many of ideas listed come from Karen Conterio and Wendy Lader, two leading national experts on self-harm.

IMMEDIATE GRATIFICATION

We currently live in a society that focuses on immediate gratification. Increasingly, our culture emphasizes a "quick fix" for even the smallest problem. This means that we are raising our children in an environment that encourages a lack of patience. Let's think about this for a moment. For most of us, taking the time to prepare a home-cooked meal often does not occur when we are busy and harassed and quite honestly, hungry. This is why we are becoming a nation of fast food. Fast food restaurants provide a quick fix solution. Unfortunately, they also foster childhood obesity. Still, most parents would agree that it is very easy to go to a drive-through, fast-food window and feed the whole family in less than ten minutes. Most of the time, we don't even wait until we get home to start eating. The first french fry or perhaps even a burger is in our mouth before the car reaches home. I am certain that if the adult driving the car was questioned about the reason for beginning dinner in the car, instead of waiting until the whole family was sitting together around the dinner table, she would say that they were hungry, hit all the red lights, and half the family was off doing other things so they wouldn't be eating together anyway. Doesn't this further illustrate the point? We are becoming increasingly impatient because we expect immediate gratification. How many of us have sat at those endless red lights and felt like we might scream if there was even one more on the way home?

If this particular example doesn't resonate for you, and illustrate how we are becoming more impatient due our desire for immediate gratification, then think about this. Television commercials have become too long for us. Tivo and My DVR were created so that we could skip through commercials and watch a whole program and several others (sometimes at the same time) in a shortened period of time. Does anyone watch live TV anymore? According to our teens, not many of them do. Along the same lines, our teens also report that when they have a feeling that is uncomfortable for them, they seek to fix it immediately through some action or behavior. This is true for adults as well, who are modeling these types of behaviors for our youth. Think about the anxious or depressed individual who reaches for an over-the-counter pill, alcoholic drink, or bag of chips. Although this behavior doesn't address the reason the person is feeling anxious or depressed, it does make the individual feel better, at least briefly. Soon, however, the individual begins to feel guilty about the behavior, and a bad feeling replaces the good one. These bad feelings that follow, as discussed earlier, can lead to the development of restricting or purging behaviors.

Unfortunately, many individuals, including our youth, view this type of "quick fix" or immediate gratification as positive and healthy. However, from these examples and our knowledge of eating disorders, I think we can see that it is not always the case. In addition to the negativity and dysfunction of unhealthy and disordered eating, another one of the main reasons that this is not always beneficial is that we are training our kids to have a very low tolerance for distress and discomfort. We see this with their impatience around many things in their lives.

DISENFRANCHISED YOUTH

The second cultural influence that underscores eating disorders in our society is the fact that our society is becoming increasingly disenfranchised. Extended family members are less available to our youth, particularly in Caucasian families, where eating disorders are the most prevalent. The collapse of the extended family, and the increasing isolation of the individual means that children have fewer confidants in times of difficulty. With more parents working outside the home, children are being raised by strangers rather than family members. Once they outgrow daycare, baby sitters and nannies take over, and latchkey children become the norm. As they become teenagers, they are raising themselves, looking for answers and guidance from their equally clueless peers. What do you think teens tell each other about what type of body looks good, will get attention, and make one popular? Certainly not an overweight, or in most cases, even an average-sized one. Instead they focus on thin and super thin. (This is not to say that only teenagers of working parents have eating disorders, but it can be a factor).

Let's go back to the example above regarding the decline of the family dinners. In the past, family dinners were considered a sacred event. It was important to families to have everyone gathered around the table at the same time to share a meal. The family dinner was the one time that family members could talk about their day and experience true feelings of togetherness. Unfortunately for many families, this ritual does not exist anymore. Someone in the family is inevitably working late, or at sports practice or a music lesson. Some kids are lucky to even sit down to a meal with their siblings and a nanny. This type of fragmented family dinner often leaves kids without a good model for healthy eating. This may be particularly true if kids are eating fast food or makeshift meals such as cereal, PB and J, and ice cream for dinner. In addition, without the entire family present, the kids have fewer people available with whom to discuss important topics.

While all conversations adults have with children are important, since this book is on eating disorders, I will focus on the importance of providing a forum for kids to discuss their thoughts and feelings about themselves and their bodies. The modern teen may grow up relying very little on words and the conventional verbal exploration of thoughts and feelings. Instead, the teen may depend more on *doing* rather than *saying*. Food is often used as a way to do something or show someone something rather than *saying or telling* someone something verbally. "I will *show* you how much I despise my body by restricting food. I will *show* you how out of control I feel by *binging and purging*.

Technology has exacerbated this problem. Our kids are turning to their friends, and their computers for information, rather than talking to their parents. Is this where we want them to get their information about food, calories, body image, and so on?

DYSFUNCTIONALITY: THE NEW COOL

The third cultural influence that supports the development of eating disorders among our youth is that our society is becoming a nation of addicts and "a-holics." Many would argue that eating disorders fit into this category. Have you noticed that it has become "in" to be considered dysfunctional? In fact, it has become so "in" that individuals volunteer to share their dysfunction with millions of viewers on national television. Think about how many people volunteer to share their dysfunctional lives on the *Oprah Winfrey Show* and how many individuals are willing to share their eating disorders with the entire nation on the *Dr. Phil Show*.

Many of our youth are hungry for attention; so hungry that they would prefer negative attention to no attention at all. What is interesting is that, when it comes to eating disorders, most teens do not see this as negative attention because they see nothing wrong with what they are doing. Teen girls think it's awesome to be thin. Thin is beautiful in our society. Girls have no problem flaunting the fact that they are getting attention for being beautiful in front of others. In fact, their greatest fantasy is to be adored by others. Most teens understand that there are no true secrets these days. In fact, often this is what saves the lives of many teen sufferers. It is usually a friend who tells a counselor or a parent that there is a problem. Without this disclosure, many more tragedies could ensue.

EMPHASIS ON THE SUPERFICIAL

Another cultural influence that leads to the development of eating disorders in our nation is that we live in a relentlessly body-focused culture where appearances are all-important and where we are encouraged by cultural imperatives to stay "on the surface of things." Researchers agree that adornment and decoration of the body are the primary means of self-expression for most cultures. Although many societies are well known for this (i.e., African tribal societies), Western society is no different. Think about how our media is saturated with commercials advertising how we can feel better about ourselves by changing our shape, diet, scent, face or bone structure (through plastic surgery), hair color, skin color (tanning) or fashion, or by buying lotions, creams, and ointments to enhance our beauty. This inevitably makes individuals, especially impressionable teenagers, feel that they are not good enough.

The media plays a role in this too. Most ads in magazines are extremely body-focused. Airbrushed models look thin and flawless, creating a complete misconception for our youth about what human beings actually look like in real life. In addition, our kids are watching movies featuring beautiful actors and actresses, and wishing they could look just like them. They are usually completely unaware that many of these movie stars use body doubles to make them look better on the big screen.

Let's not forget about television and T.V. commercials. These forms of media also focus on physical beauty, and insinuate that you will be happier if you are thin. In addition, persistent and debilitating gender biases are driving our young female teens to more severe emotional extremes than ever before. Eating disorders are just one way that girls will go to great lengths to express their fear, frustration, anger, and disgust with themselves and their bodies.

Lader and Conterio explain that as long as human beings have existed, they have used the skin to communicate identity, status and any number of other characteristics such as political preference, sexual orientation, etc. These symbolizations of the self are advertised through body art – tattoos, piercing, cutting - much like a bumper sticker on a car. The anorexic's emaciated body is also an advertisement. If asked, many of these individuals would probably state that it illustrates their hard work, achievement and perfectionism. Many cultures (primitive and modern) have used tribal markings to unite their community and imbue a sense of belonging. (e.g., Hindu women: red dot; Native American tribes: facial decorations, markings; street gangs: tattoos, colors). For the anorexic individual, their skeletal frame provides something similar. Unfortunately, the anorexic's tribal marking can be lethal.

ONLINE INFLUENCES AND THE DANGERS OF GROUP THINK

So how can we prevent our youth from developing this aggressive and deadly illness despite the many adverse influences in our society? Intervention is key. Many individuals who struggle with an ED will seek treatment in an inpatient setting. Although different types of treatment will be more thoroughly explored in the chapter on intervention and recovery, I would like to mention something of importance here that has to do with prevention.

Medical and mental health professionals agree that when eating disorder patients are in recovery programs, they often join together and discuss their signs and symptoms as a way to gain emotional support and validation for their struggles. Although this can be a positive influence at times, it can also become a negative if they use this contact to share tricks that will help them maintain their illness. Most commonly, individuals with anorexia collectively try to minimize their symptoms and normalize their condition. They will defend their illness by claiming that it is not one. Instead they convince themselves, and in turn, one another, that it is an accomplishment. I have had several patients tell me that they justify the restriction of food as a learned trait of self-control. This is something they are proud of and would never want to change. In fact, they see it as an integral part of their identity. To take this away from them would be a loss of self.

One way that eating-disordered individuals identify themselves to one another is through the use of bracelets. Red bracelets are often worn by pro-anorexia teens as a discreet way to recognize other people in social situations who are struggling with anorexia. It is also a constant reminder to avoid eating when out with friends and family. Blue and purple bracelets are often worn by pro-bulimia teenagers for similar reasons.

PRO-EATING DISORDER WEBSITES

Treatment programs are not the only place we are seeing eating-disordered patients band together to pro-mote their illness. With growing technology and use of the internet, our teens are going online to gain this sup-port. Advocating for an illness that is potentially lethal is ludicrous, I know. However, ED-specific websites and chat rooms are now available with a click of a mouse.

Pro-eating disorder websites were first created in the 1990's. In the past decade, however, they have become much more popular. This increase in popularity is related to the increase in blogging and social networking sites that children are utilizing. Web forums and sites such Face-book, Myspace, LiveJournal, and Xanga are extremely popular among our teens. They provide support through online groups which are sought out by individuals who are isolating from friends and family. For these teens, online social networking is often the only social outlet that they have. Not surprisingly, research shows it is much more common for females to join these groups (chat rooms) than males.

As mentioned above, individuals who go on these sites and join these groups often advocate for the illness and support the maintenance of both anorexia and bulimia.

The pro-anorexia websites are often referred to as pro-ana sites and the pro-bulimia websites are often referred to as pro-mia.

Below I have listed examples of the kind of information your child may gather by visiting these sites:

❋ The latest crash diets (including low calorie meal recipes)

❋ How to manage or decrease hunger pains (e.g. chewing gum, drinking water, etc.)

❋ How to trick people into thinking you are eating when you are not (e.g., how to move food around on your plate and/or hide it in your clothing to dispose of it later when nobody is looking).

❋ Tips on hiding weight loss from family, friends, and doctors (e.g. wear layers of clothing to hide emaciation, tape weights to your skin under your underwear so not be detected by the doctor, water logging before a weigh in, etc.)

❋ Advice on how to induce vomiting and how to get the best results from using diuretics and laxatives.

❋ Tips on how to flatten your stomach (e.g., wrap yourself with cling wrap or a bandage before you go to bed at night).

In addition, your child may be enticed by the following:

❋ Encouragement to participate in a "biggest loser" contest among other group members (this is a weight loss competition).

- Encouragement to fast with other members as a way to unite together in their fight to be thin. This is often referred to as "thinspiration"
- Encouragement to post their weight, body measurements, and pictures of themselves to inspire one another ("thinspiration").
- Encouragement to share their meal plans and results to promote their weight loss and gain affirmation ("thinspiration").
- Encouragement to purge following a binge or breaking a fast.
- Encouragement to post old photos of self prior to eating disorder (if overweight or obese). This is intended to scare the person about returning to their past weight and to motivate further weight loss. through restricting/purging/fasting/over-exercising. Other viewers are motivated by the disgust they feel when viewing these pictures of obese or overweight individuals. This is referred to as "reverse thinspiration."

Once a child is diagnosed with an ED, they visit the pro-eating disorder sites to prolong their illness. This means that your child is enlisting a community of other eating-disordered teens to support their illness. In 2006, Stanford Medical School conducted a study of individuals who were diagnosed with an eating disorder. Researchers wanted to find out the level of participation in pro-eating disorder websites among patients. Results indicated that 35% of the individuals had visited a pro-ana website. Out of those individuals, 96% learned new weight loss techniques to maintain their illness including purging methods.

PRO-ED WEBSITES AND NON-ED KIDS

I think the most important thing for parents to keep in mind about pro-ED websites in the prevention stage is that they are often visited by non-eating disordered teenagers who are seeking tips on dieting and weight loss. Clearly the tips they will receive by visiting these sites are highly detrimental and can encourage disordered eating. In a 2009, CyberSentinel, a parental control software vendor, conducted a study of 1500 female Internet users aged six to fifteen. Results indicated that one in three of the girls reported having searched online for dieting tips. In addition, one in five of the girls reported having corresponded with others on social networking sites or in chat rooms for tips on dieting.

Further studies were conducted to gain information about the effect of viewing these sites. In 2006, The University of Missouri conducted an experimental study with 235 female undergraduates. Results indicated that the females subjected to a single viewing of a pro-ana site reported lower self-esteem and a preoccupation with weight loss and exercise as compared to individuals who were in the control group. In addition, there was a greater likelihood for the individuals in the study to exercise, and a reduced likelihood to overeat.

I know I have spent a lot of time talking about the importance of communicating with your kids on the topic of healthy eating and healthy body image. Remember one of the most effective ways to prevent the development of an eating disorder is to identify emerging symptoms early. Identification can occur through observation, through communication or through a combination of both. Communicating to your child your concerns about observable emerging symptoms could, in and of itself, prevent the onset of an ED. However if communication ends up not being enough, then we have to move into the intervention phase. In the next two chapters, we will explore treatment and intervention in great detail.

4

OVERCOMING
RESISTANCE AND
ENTERING TREATMENT

If, through your own assessment or that of a professional, you determine that your child has developed an
eating disorder and prevention is no longer an option, you
must move to the intervention phase. As noted earlier,
parents should expect their child to resist entering
therapy. Most of the time, the individual does not think
there is a problem. If the individual is anorexic, it is likely
that for the past several months, all she has been hearing is
how wonderful she looks. We live in a society where
weight loss is desirable and body image ideals are those of
models and movie stars. And, as discussed, AN causes distorted thinking and an intense fear of gaining weight.

If the individual is bulimic, it is likely that for the past several months or even years, (remember this eating disorder is less detectible since it is generally not associated with sudden weight loss), she has heard nothing to indicate that there is a problem. With no indication that something is wrong, it seems ridiculous to enter treatment. After all, most people with BN are not starving and "look" just fine. In some cases, however, the person with bulimia has some concerns.

Because the act of binging and purging is seen as disgusting, gross, and "unnatural," the person is often highly embarrassed and ashamed of her behavior. This is different from the person with AN who restricts food to lose weight. Restricting food seems much more "civilized," "normal," and "clean." In fact, it is an accomplishment that many people in our society are proud of and hold in high regard. A person with the willpower to avoid fattening foods and stay on a diet is envied. Do you know anyone in our society who is envied or held in high regard for throwing up all the time? Accordingly, the person with BN does not speak about her behavior because she believes people will think of her negatively. Unfortunately, this leads to even greater resistance to entering treatment.

The sooner the person starts treatment, the higher the rate of success. If your child has AN, explain to her that getting help does not mean getting fat. The goals of treatment are to help the individual see herself accurately, so that there are no more distortions, and to find alternative coping mechanisms that will provide healthier outlets for distress. If your child has BN, explain to her that getting help means dealing with the distress in her life alternatively. The person with BN is not afraid of "getting fat" because she engages in compensatory methods to alleviate this fear. Therefore, the goals of treatment are to help her break the cycle of binging and then purging/fasting/over-exercising.   In the case of both AN and BN, understanding why this illness developed in the first place is imperative so that it does not return or be replaced by another unhealthy coping mechanism. Therefore, treatment will also focus on understanding and identifying triggers to the onset of this illness.

In general, clients with eating disorders are often mistrustful of authority figures, including medical and mental health professionals. This is particularly true for anorexic patients, since they often deny their illness and wish to be left alone. They usually do not seek treatment of their own volition, but instead end up in therapy under protest, feeling coerced by a concerned family member or friend.   They enter therapy prepared to fight treatment, not cooperate with it.   The anorexic patient often views the therapist as an enemy who will try to make them eat, which would be the ultimate loss of personal control. The bulimic patient is often terrified that her therapist will judge her. Since she is often embarrassed by her behavior and feels ashamed that she cannot stop the cycle of binging and purging/fasting/over-exercising, entering therapy causes her to feel significant guilt and fear about how she will be judged.

BUILDING A THERAPEUTIC ALLIANCE

Given this initial atmosphere of guilt, fear and distrust, it is imperative to choose a therapist who can overcome these obstacles and create an environment of safety, comfort and support for your child. Finding the right therapist is not always easy. However, it is a critical first step that will optimize the chances of successful treatment.

I strongly believe that therapy is only as successful as the "Goodness of Fit," between the therapist and the patient. In order for the therapeutic work to be successful, the therapist must build an alliance with the client. If the level of comfort and trust necessary to build this alliance is not present, help your child find a different therapist. Changing therapists does not represent a failure on the therapist's part or the child's part. It simply means there may not be a good fit, which is necessary for successful treatment and recovery. In fact, research has proven that having a strong therapeutic alliance is the most important factor in successful treatment. In numerous studies, this was ranked above type of therapy (theoretical approach), and counselor training/experience.

It is very important for the therapist to be patient and non-critical with the client. Following the client's lead is also imperative, because it reinforces to the client that she is in charge of her treatment. The moment the therapist takes a confrontational stance or leads the client, she will feel the therapist is attempting to control her and will either resist treatment or terminate.

EXPLAINING THAT TREATMENT IS MANDATORY

While your child may help choose a particular therapist based on whether he or she feels comfortable with that professional, kids struggling with eating disorders should **never** have a choice about attending treatment. Parents should make it very clear to their child that they must be involved in some type of therapeutic intervention.

It is appropriate to explain to your child why she has no choice in this matter. Explain that you love her and that you are very concerned for both her physical and mental well-being. Tell her that without treatment, you are afraid she might die and that you are NOT going to let that happen because part of your job as a parent is keeping your child safe. Tell her that it would be neglectful and uncaring for you to allow her to avoid treatment intervention.

To help make this last premise clear to children, I suggest that parents use the following analogy:

"If you had cancer, I would not sit around and do nothing about it. It would be ludicrous for me **not** to set up an appointment with a doctor and begin some sort of treatment immediately, especially knowing that without treatment you would inevitably die. An eating disorder is not that different from cancer. It is a serious illness that needs to be treated aggressively. Therefore, I am not going to wait and see if things get better on their own. I love you and care about you too much to let anything bad happen to you."

After hearing these things from their parent(s), most kids will begin therapy, even if begrudgingly. Do not expect your child to jump for joy after hearing these words, and suddenly be highly motivated to get well. These words are usually very meaningful for kids and are often remembered and discussed later in treatment. However, in that initial moment, they will never admit it to you.

SPECIFIC STRATEGIES TO OVERCOME RESISTANCE

Some kids continue to resist treatment even after hearing these words from their parent(s). If your child continues to resist treatment remember this: *No matter how much they beg and plead, you must stay strong and reiterate that attending treatment is not a choice.* Be prepared for your child in her state of resistance to try to convince you that (1) there is no problem, (2) you caused the problem and if you force her into treatment you will make it worse, (3) you are the only one with a problem so why don't you go to therapy instead, (4) she can fix the problem on her own so don't waste your money on someone she doesn't even want to see in the first place (5) if you make her go to treatment she will only sit there and won't talk, so it will be a waste of time and money, and (6) if you make her go to treatment, she will run away or even worse try to kill herself.

In the event that you are confronted with some of these statements, I thought it would be helpful to talk about each of them separately and provide ideas as to how to respond.

There is no problem!

Suggested response: "If that is true, then I will be so relieved. In fact, I really hope that there isn't anything to worry about. I love you so much and I don't want anything to happen to you. However, I am not an expert on eating disorders and I can't make that determination. If you had signs and symptoms of cancer, I would not try to assess if you actually had this illness myself. Instead, I would take you to an oncologist, who specializes in cancer, and wait for their determination." This often drives the point home to your child that she has a very serious illness that needs immediate attention.

You caused the problem and if you force me into treatment you will make it worse!

This statement almost always makes parents feel defensive. Unfortunately, becoming defensive does not help the situation. It is important to acknowledge your child's feelings. You may completely disagree with what she is saying, but remember it is how *she is feeling* and *she is sharing* these feelings with you. The worst thing to do is to dismiss her feelings and/or to tell her that her perception of the problem is wrong. People have different perceptions. A trained practitioner will address this in treatment. For now, your daughter is willing to open up to you, so do not shut her down. If you do, she will most likely not share her feelings openly and honestly with you again. The suggested response below acknowledges her feelings:

"I am so sorry if you believe that I am the cause of the problem. I am sure there have been things that I have done that have led you to feel this way. It was never my intent to do anything to hurt you or to trigger your problems with eating. I am glad that you told me that you feel this way. I am convinced now, more than ever, that we need to set up some therapeutic appointments. Maybe we need to go to the first therapy session together so we can talk more about this. Perhaps we can also find a family therapist to help us because I certainly do not want to keep doing things that contribute to your restricting/ binging/purging."

By stating that you are willing to attend sessions with her and set up some family therapy appointments, you are showing her that she will not have to enter treatment and recovery alone. In other words, you are declaring that you are "in it together" as a family. This type of statement is very powerful for kids even if they do not admit it at the time. Many of them do indeed talk about this later in treatment and say that it was one of the driving forces that helped them work in treatment to get better.

You are the one with a problem, so why don't you go to therapy instead!

I have found that the best way to respond to this is very similar to the response listed immediately above ("You caused the problem and if you force me into treatment you will make it worse!"). It is important to remain neutral and to try not to become defensive. In part, your child may be saying this to make you angry. She may also be saying it to deflect the focus off of her and to place it on you.   Parents often fall for this tactic.   They become enraged that their child is insinuating they have a problem when clearly she is the one with the problem.   In the heat of the moment, an argument often erupts, with the parents responding angrily, "I am not the one who refuses to eat food; I am not the one who is killing herself, I am not the one who is destroying the family, etc."

Not only are these statements not helpful, they are counterproductive and psychologically detrimental. Your child will walk away feeling even worse about herself and move deeper into her eating disorder mentality and behavior.   Instead, validate your child's feelings and make a statement that you are willing to attend therapy sessions with her to help resolve the problem.

I can fix the problem on my own so don't waste your money on someone I don't want to see in the first place!

Suggested response: "I am glad that you feel strong enough to overcome this problem on your own.   I know that if you put your mind to it and work really hard you will overcome this problem.   However, I am not sure if you can do it alone and that has nothing to do with you. This is a very aggressive illness that needs to be treated aggressively.   I have learned that it is very difficult to over-come an eating disorder without the support of a medical team and your family.   To tell you the truth, I don't even know if I would want you to try to do it on your own.   I love you and I want to learn how I can help you.   I want to

find an expert that has worked with individuals and families and can tell us what we can do to support you through
treatment and recovery."

When addressing the issue of money, each family has
different financial circumstances and will need to make
decisions accordingly.   There are wonderful experts that
may be in-network with insurance companies so that
therapy sessions would involve only a co-pay.   There are
also wonderful experts who work in private practice and
are often out-of-network providers.   Families must work
with their insurance companies to determine reimbursement, and decide what treatment options are feasible.
Some families do not want to go through their insurance
companies at all.   In this case, the full fee of the practitioner would be out of pocket with no reimbursement.   In
any case, the best way to try to respond to the money issue
is to say that you will find an option that works for your
family so that your child can get the help that she needs.

If you make me go to treatment, I will sit there and I won't talk; so it will be a waste of your time and money!

I cannot begin to tell you how many kids say this to their
parents, causing the parents to call me in a panic believing
that therapy will now be useless.   I assure parents that
although kids often say this, it is usually not the case.   In
fact, most kids have a very hard time sitting in complete
silence. It feels awkward for them. Isn't this true for most
people? It is exceptionally rare to have even an extremely
resistant child come to my office and not speak at all.   In

part, this is due to the fact that most therapists are trained
and highly skilled in helping kids feel comfortable so that
they are able to open up and disclose personal information. Therefore, I have found that one of the best ways to
respond to this statement is to say something like this:

"I really hope that you are able to talk to the person
that you choose to work with. I know it is not always easy
to open up and be honest about a problem you are facing,
but you are strong. I believe that if you do find a way
to open up and talk, you will be tremendously successful.
It takes a lot of courage to go to counseling and I believe
that working on oneself and overcoming a problem is
never a waste of time or money."

The first sentence reinforces the fact that your child has
a choice in who she sees. It also insinuates that she will be
attending therapy no matter what.   The rest of the
response provides your child with support and positive
reinforcement to get the help she needs. The last sentence
addresses 'the waste of time and money,' comment by
placing value on the therapy, which is important for her to
hear from her parents.

There are a lot of parents who do not believe in
therapy. You may be one of them. Kids are very
aware when a parent looks down upon treatment. In
fact, often continued resistance from a child to be in
therapy comes from the modeling of a parent. They are
quick to tell their therapist that their parent thinks "all psy-
chologists are quacks." Everyone has a right to their
opinion, just be mindful that if you have this opinion, your
child is likely to adopt it as well, and not engage in

the therapy that she needs to help her overcome her problem.

If you make me go to treatment, I will run away or even worse I will try to kill myself!

This is probably a parent's worst nightmare. You may find it hard to believe that your child would say something like this, however, it is actually very common statement made out of desperation by kids faced with treatment. I have found that one of the best responses to this type of statement is this:

"I love you and could never imagine life without you. This must be so scary for you to say something like that. To even think about hurting yourself or taking your life tells me how scary this must be for you. I know you don't want to be in therapy, but it is incredibly important for us to get you some help."

You can then use several of the other statement listed in the responses above. You can talk about it being neglectful to not get her into treatment. You can make the analogy to cancer. You can offer to attend some sessions with her. You can let her know that she will have the ability to choose the right therapist for her. All of these things are incredibly helpful.

What is not helpful is backing down in response to her threat, and avoiding treatment. However, safety always comes first and I am not implying that you should ignore her statement of harm and/or potential suicide. In fact, parents should take this very seriously. You may want to watch her 24/7 until you have confirmation from her therapist that she is not suicidal and can be safely left alone.

If she continues to make threats of harm or suicide and you do not feel like you can keep her safe, you may want to bring her to the closest emergency room where psychiatric personnel will evaluate her for safety. If it determined that she is a danger to herself, she may be hospitalized. If this is the case, she will be placed on a "5150," which is a 72-hour hold. The hospital will most likely transfer her to an adolescent psychiatric unit where she will be monitored by medical and mental health practitioners until they determine that she is no longer at risk and can return home. Often the person returns home within the 72 hours, but if she continues to be a danger to herself (according to subjective report or behavioral observation), then she will be kept longer.

I wish that dealing with these convincing arguments to avoid treatment were all that parents were up against. Unfortunately, once parents have overcome this hurdle they are often faced with another one. Parents often ask me on the day of the initial appointment, "How do I get my child to come in to see you?" or "What do I say to her, because she is refusing to go?" Many parents feel helpless in getting their child into treatment. It is common for parents to call me on the phone prior to an appointment and ask "What if she refuses to get into the car?" Some parents will say "I cannot drag her into the car and make her come, can I?" Obviously, this indicates that the child with the problem is very powerful in the family. I encourage parents to be firm and loving and not to take no for an answer. Below I have listed some things that I often guide parents to say to their child when in this type of situation.

❋ Remember that you have a choice in who you see. If you do not like this person, then we will interview some other therapists. Please give it a try.

❋ If you are unable to attend outpatient therapy because you are refusing to go to appointment, then we will have to start looking at either a day treatment program or a residential program where you will not have a choice to go because it is built into the program.

❋ Let's just get in the car and drive over there. If you still refuse, then you refuse. Once you are at the office, you can ask the therapist to come out to the car for the initial appointment. This is something most therapists will do.

❋ I will go with you to the first meeting if you would like. I am here to support you even though you don't want to go.

❋ If you don't go to the appointment, then you will not be able to go over to your friend's house tonight, the concert on Friday, your voice lessons, etc.

5

INTERVENTION AND RECOVERY

COMMUNICATING WITH YOUR CHILD: A GUIDE FOR PARENTS AND CAREGIVERS

Since we have spent a lot of time emphasizing the importance of communication with our kids, it is useful to discuss how to have positive and healthy discussions with them. Most child experts will advise parents to try to be open, honest and good listeners when talking with their children. What they don't say, however, is how hard that can be, especially when the child is your own and the topic is a tough one like eating disorders. Maybe, like most parents, you don't know where to start. In addition, you don't want to sound critical, rude or oblivious. I have already listed some ways for parents to approach their child when asking assessment questions. I would like to add some additional tips below. I would also like to refer you to a wonderful book called *Help Your Teen Beat an Eating Disorder*, written by James Lock, M.D., Ph.D. and Daniel Le Grange, Ph.D. Their book does a brilliant job of supporting parents and guiding them in exactly what they can do when their child has been diagnosed with this devastating illness.

Here are some additional tips for parents when talking with your child following determination that they have an eating disorder.

1. A caregiver should be calm and non-judgmental when talking about the ED. This does not mean that the caregiver should not acknowledge the damaging and dangerous nature of the behavior, but it does mean that the way in which this message is conveyed should not make the child feel rejected, scolded or criticized.

2. The ideal caregiver should be firm, open-minded and empathetic. A non-judgmental attitude toward the child and her behavior must be portrayed at all times. Anything other than a neutral stance will inevitably lead to less success in recovery.

3. Spouses must be on the same page. Present as a united front. If one caregiver says one thing and the other says another, the eating disorder will take advantage of the inconsistency and go with the less-firm parent.

4. Lend Support – Do not hesitate to help your child fight again the negative thoughts that lead to the ED

behavior. *Note: it does not work to fight against your child; it does work to fight against the illness. Also do not hesitate to encourage or suggest alternative behaviors (i.e. take your child on a walk, go to the movies, etc).

5. The greatest resource for your child is YOU!!! Don't minimize the amount of influence you have over your child.

6. Help your child to re-feed or stop the binge/purge cycle. Reinforcing the need to eat and not overeat/purge can be vitally important and helpful to your child. However, this cannot be done in a critical way. Use words that focus on the illness being the problem and not on the child being the problem.

7. Help your child see that she is more than an ED. Helping her understand and see that her identity is separate from the ED is paramount. It is hard to fight against yourself; it is much easier to fight against a behavior.

THE DIFFICULT ROAD TO RECOVERY

It is not easy to recover from an eating disorder. As discussed earlier, eating disorders affect both the mind and the body. Therefore, treatment must include intervention for both. In our society, having a certain body image is ideal and desired. Most women strive to "look good" on a daily basis. However, anyone who has ever struggled with an eating disorder knows that an eating disorder never really allows a person to "feel good." In fact, it is usually the opposite. The person often feels ugly and unworthy, which leads to a stronger desire to lose weight. Unfortunately, the more weight the person loses, the more distorted her body image becomes. The person feels defeated and hopeless. And what may have started out as a simple diet has become a debilitating disease.

As I mentioned earlier in the chapter on AN, having a distorted body image is possibly the cruelest part of the disease. Because it does not permit the sufferer to have an accurate perception of the body, it causes confusion and frustration when others view her as very thin while she sees herself as overweight. The eating-disordered person is not "crazy," she is simply malnourished. A malnourished brain causes body distortion. In fact, the thinner the person becomes, the more distortion she may experience. Without treatment, the desire to attain that "perfect body" (the one that they will never be able to see through eating-disordered eyes) becomes stronger.

Individuals with BN typically do not experience body distortion. This is likely due to the fact that they are typically average or slightly above average weight for their height. Even those individuals who may be somewhat below average weight for their height are typically not suffering from the extreme malnourishment that leads to body distortion. Therefore, they do not experience the same confusion as the individual with AN about entering treatment. However, they do experience their own frustration when others view them as having a problem that nobody can visibly see. They are not skeletally thin, as AN patients are, and they know it. Since they are not "starving themselves" they often do not believe that they are doing any harm to their bodies, and thus do not see why they should enter treatment. However, without treatment, the cycle of binging and then purging/fasting/over-exercising typically intensifies and becomes much more dangerous.

One of the reasons that eating disorders are considered particularly difficult to treat is the uncertainty about the underlying cause or causes. Accordingly, in order to set up a proper treatment plan, all potential causes must be explored with the child. This, in and of itself, may pose a problem since eating disorders are considered to be 'ego-syntonic.' This means that the person suffering from the illness often does not think there is anything wrong with what she is doing and therefore, does not want any help. Psychological disorders that are ego-dystonic, such as depression and/or anxiety, are problems that the person very much wants to resolve. The person views these disorders as unpleasant, uncomfortable, and often distressing. Accordingly, their motivation to enter treatment and alleviate the problem is high. Conversely, patients with eating disorders (ego-syntonic) have low motivation for therapy.

This low motivation may also reflect the fact that treatment for an eating disorder is complicated and often long-term. In addition, professionals vary in their opinions about the best psychological treatment approach, treatment modality, and treatment setting for the eating-disordered patient, which can lead to frustration and confusion. One thing that professionals do tend to agree upon is the use of a collaborative team in the treatment of the eating-disordered patient. (See more on this below under the heading Treatment: A Multi-Disciplinary Approach).

It takes a lot of courage to embark in recovery from an eating disorder. It is not an easy process. Unlike recovery from other addictions, where the person can stay away from the addictive substance (such as alcohol or drugs), the person cannot stay away from food. Can you imagine asking an alcoholic or gambler to recover from their addiction while still having to drink or go to the racetrack up to three times a day? The good news is that there are wonderful treatments available with specialists who can help in the recovery process.

TREATMENT: A MULTI-DISCIPLINARY APPROACH

Traditionally, the treatment of AN has taken place in the inpatient setting with the main treatment goal focusing on weight restoration. Weight restoration usually occurs within one to 14 weeks. Once the individual's weight is stable, the person leaves the inpatient setting and begins treatment in an outpatient setting. This is usually where the person begins to work on the "mind" aspect of the illness since the "body" aspect is now in recovery. As long as the person's weight remains stable, the focus will remain on this aspect of recovery.

Treatment for BN has traditionally not taken place in an inpatient setting, since the sufferer typically is not in need of weight restoration. However, more recently, this starting point has been increasingly utilized due to the person's medical instability (i.e. electrolyte imbalances or heart arrhythmias). The treatment focus in the inpatient setting for the individual with BN is not only on regaining medical stability, but on breaking the habit of the bulimic cycle. Often the individual needs the structure of the inpatient setting and the strict monitoring of hospital staff to make a behavioral shift successfully.

Once the individual's vital signs are stable, the person leaves the inpatient setting and begins treatment in an outpatient setting. This occurs even if the person does not feel "ready" to leave due to their lack of success in breaking the bulimic cycle. As is the case with the anorexic patient, once the bulimic patient enters outpatient treatment, she begins to work on the "mind" aspect of the illness. The "body" aspect of the illness receives continued focus as wel,l since the urges to binge and then purge/fast/over-exercise are still very strong.

The psycho-educational approach to treatment requires a multi-disciplinary team. Both anorexic and bulimic patients should be working with a team of professionals, including a medical doctor, nutritionist, and therapist. The medical doctor's job is to monitor medical stability and ensure medical safety. The nutritionist's job is to set up a meal plan, and educate both the child and her parents about food, nutrition, and calories.

Both the nutritionist and medical doctor should be educated about the specific treatment of eating disorders. For example, some doctors are not aware that when checking an anorexic's blood pressure, three measures are necessary to ensure medical stability. Measures need to be assessed while the client is lying down, then while sitting down, and then while standing up. Their blood pressure may change drastically during these measures. Failure to properly assess blood pressure can put an eating-disordered client at serious risk.

Furthermore, when assessing clients with anorexia, it is important to know that they share psychological and behavioral characteristics with people who are faced with starvation. These characteristics include: pre-occupation with food, food hoarding, slow eating, disturbances in gastric emptying, binge eating, cognitive changes, moodiness, apathy, irritability, decreased libido, and sleep disturbances. These characteristics demonstrate the strong need for nutritional rehabilitation and reinforce the need for a multi-disciplinary team approach.

In the case of the person with BN, some doctors are not trained in how to determine whether the person is purging. There is a simple and painless examination of the mouth that can alert the doctor to this behavior. In addition, doctors should be testing blood to check for electrolyte imbalances and the use of over-the-counter and/or prescription and non-prescription drugs to elicit weight loss after a binge. The habitual nature of binging followed by compensatory methods can lead to dangerous outcomes. It is for this reason that a multi-disciplinary team approach is vital.

THE THERAPIST'S ROLE IN TREATMENT

The therapist's role is to work on the psychological components of the illness and help the patient move toward recovery. Psychotherapy is considered to be a crucial component of the treatment plan. There are several theories as to why a child engages in unhealthy eating patterns leading to the development of an eating disorder. Below is a list of some of them.

* Fear of growing up and becoming independent (AN)
* Physical way to handle chaos and feelings of being overwhelmed (BN)
* Fear of failure and fear of success (AN and BN)
* Way to get attention/become noticed (AN more common)
* Take attention off something else in the family system that is distressing e.g. parent conflict (AN and BN)
* Feel more in control (AN and BN)

Often in the course of therapy, these theories are explored with the child who is suffering. This exploration is done in a way that helps the child understand and is adjusted to their level of insight, maturity, and development.

The therapist working with your child should do several important things during the course of treatment.

* <u>Set up a treatment participation agreement</u> - This is a collaborative process. Decisions should be made together. The agreement can be written (formal) or verbal (informal).
* <u>Create mutually agreed-upon goals</u> - Goals should be objective and attainable.
* <u>Include a written contract</u> - The goal here is not only to avoid the ED behavior, but also to increase the window of opportunity between the time the patient feels the

urge to restrict/binge and then purge/fast/over-exercise, and the actual act of restricting/binging and then purging/fasting/over-exercising. When things are put in writing and signed by both the therapist and the patient, the patient often feels more obligated to follow through with their formal commitment.

❋ Have the medical doctor regularly assess the need for hospitalization – Remember safety comes first.

❋ Provide a confidential, non-judgmental environment for your child to discuss her eating disorder - Ideally she will feel free to discuss all aspects of her life and how they connect to her eating disorder.

TYPES OF TREATMENT

There are many kinds of both individual and family therapy. While it is not possible to cover all of them, I have detailed two different approaches that I have used with great success for many years. Individual therapy is addressed in chapter 6 and family therapy is addressed in chapter 7.

6

INDIVIDUAL THERAPY

INTRODUCTION TO CBT AND INSIGHT-ORIENTED THERAPY

Two types of theoretical approaches often used in individual therapy are Cognitive Behavioral Therapy (CBT) and Insight-Oriented Therapy. Both are research-based approaches that have been proven successful in the treatment of eating disorders. As noted in the last chapter, there are many different kinds of theoretical approaches utilized by mental health workers when treating an individual with an ED. In this chapter, I will focus on the approaches I have used successfully with hundreds of patients for almost two decades.

I use a combination of CBT and insight-oriented therapy. I first began using CBT when treating eating disorder patients due to the many clinically significant findings that this type of therapy yields high success rates. I

later added insight-oriented work and treated patients
with a combination of the two different types of therapy.
The insight-oriented work helps my patients better understand the reasons for the onset of their illness and aids in
relapse prevention.

COGNITIVE BEHAVIORAL THERAPY (CBT)

When a patient first enters outpatient therapy, I begin
by using CBT. CBT is a psychotherapeutic approach that
seeks to address dysfunctional cognitions, emotions, and
behaviors through a goal-oriented, systematic procedure.
There is empirical evidence that CBT is effective in the
treatment of a variety of problems, including eating disorders. CBT merges cognitive therapy and behavioral
therapy, which is why it seems to work so well for individuals suffering from the psychological and physiological
components of an eating disorder. CBT focuses on the
"here and now," and on alleviating symptoms, which is the
reason for starting with this type of therapy when the
patient first enters counseling.

Often parents are told what type of therapy a doctor
will utilize when working with their child, however, they
often do not understand what that treatment entails.
Accordingly, I would like to provide a description of CBT
treatment. One of the first things that a therapist might do
when utilizing CBT is to help the patient make a connection between her thoughts, feelings, and behavior(s). The
behavior(s) for a person diagnosed with an ED would be
restricting, binging, purging, and/or over-exercising.

In order to do this, the therapist usually starts by helping the patient identify an antecedent event that leads to the cyclical process, and ultimately ends in ED behavior. I like to draw a diagram to act as a visual aid when helping patients figure this process out. Below is the diagram I draw for my patients when I make this intervention.

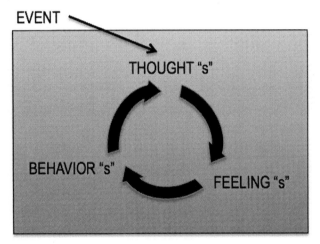

Cycling Process

I explain the diagram to them by first pointing to the word EVENT. I explain that an event is anything that happens outside of the person. It can be good or bad, right or wrong (the therapist should not judge this). I then explain that often people connect events with feelings. For example, let's say the event is getting an 'A' on a test. The person receiving this grade would probably feel happy. She might even tell people, "I am feeling so excited because I got an 'A' on my biology test." The problem with this is that the event did not cause the person to feel this way. It was their thoughts about the event that caused her to feel this way. However, most people are unaware of this and therefore connect their feelings to the event.

Let's look at another example. Say two people, a boy and a girl, get accepted into Columbia University. They both experience the same event; getting into a highly prestigious school. The girl is extremely excited and very happy about her acceptance. She makes the connection between the event and her feelings and tells everyone that she is ecstatic because she got into Columbia. The problem is that it is *not* the event that caused her to feel this way. It was her thoughts about the event that led to her feelings of happiness. So what was she thinking? She was thinking that she wanted to go. After all, Columbia was her number one choice of school. Her feelings of excitement and joy then led to certain behaviors. Her smile stretched from ear to ear, and she hugged everyone around her.

Now let's look at the boy. He experienced the same exact event; getting into Columbia University. However, he was extremely upset about his acceptance. If an event causes us to feel a certain way, then he should have had the same feelings as the girl. However, we now know that an event does not cause us to feel a certain way, it is our thoughts about an event that cause us to feel a certain way. So what was he thinking? He was thinking, "I don't want to go to Columbia University. My mother and father went there and so did my three older brothers. In addition, my sister is there right now. I want to go to NYU instead, but I was forced to apply to Columbia and now I am going to get all kinds of pressure to attend that school." These thoughts (and he had many) led to his feelings of sadness, anger, frustration, and worry. His feelings, which were very different from the girl's, led to very different behaviors. He did not smile or hug everyone around him. Conversely, he voiced his feelings to his parents, slammed his bedroom door, and turned his music to full blast.

Probably one of the most important things to know about CBT and this cycle of events leading to thoughts and then to feelings and then to behaviors, is that it does not stop with one full cycle but continues in this cyclical fashion multiple times throughout a day. For example, the boy had thoughts about his behavior (voicing his feelings, slamming his door, and blasting music). Perhaps he thought "they must know how much I don't want to go and maybe won't put pressure on me now that they see how upset I am" or "I am in big trouble for yelling at my parents and slamming my door." In either case, these thoughts lead to more feelings and more behaviors, which in turn lead to more thoughts, feelings, and behaviors.

There are only two places in this cycle where therapeutic intervention can take place. I often circle them for the patient to illustrate these points of change. Cognitions and behavior can be altered. Events are not easily altered because many of them are out of our control. We do not have control over other people's actions for example. We may be able to influence a person's behavior to some extent, however, people are ultimately responsible for their own actions. It is also not easy to alter feelings. Has anyone ever come up to you when you were angry or upset about something and told you to "get over it?" Not only does this invalidate your feelings, but it is usually almost impossible to do. If it were easy to "get over your feelings" then most people would. Most people don't want to feel angry or upset about something. They would much prefer to feel happy. So how does one change their feelings? By altering their thoughts. Remember, it is our thoughts about an event that causes us to feel a certain way. Therefore, focusing on our cognitions and changing them in some way will lead to a change in our emotions and then a change in our behavior.

Changing thoughts and behaviors becomes the focus in therapy when utilizing CBT. The therapist will help the patient identify her thoughts and list them on a piece of paper. I call these thoughts unproductive thoughts. They are also known as irrational thoughts. The reason I call them unproductive versus irrational is because some of them may actually be rational/logical. However, this does not mean that they are helpful or productive. Unproductive thoughts need to be challenged in order to be changed. Accordingly, the therapist helps the patient come up with challenges to their unproductive thoughts in an attempt to shift their thinking and halt the cycle leading to the ED behavior.

For the person with an eating disorder, the behavior to be changed is restricting, binging, purging, and/or over-exercising. In order to halt the cycle leading to these behaviors, the therapist must go backwards in the cycle and help the patient to identify their feelings first, then their thoughts, and then a triggering event. I often start by asking the patient what they were feeling right before they engaged in the ED behavior. Often the response is fear. It is also common for the person to be feeling sad, angry and confused. The person can usually identify where their feelings come from and connect them to an event. However, as we have established, it is not an event that causes a person to feel a certain way, but rather their thoughts about that event. I educate the person on this and then help them to identify their thoughts about the event. These thoughts are then challenged as noted above.

Let's take a look at this example. I was working with a patient who had been in recovery for several weeks. She called me for an emergency appointment after a relapse with binging and purging. When she came into the office we talked about what happened. She said that she was out to dinner with her friends at a Mexican restaurant and had "pigged out" on nachos, quesadillas and tacos. She felt physically ill from eating so much food and "completely freaked out." She said that she had not felt that full since she was in the depths of her eating disorder a few months ago. She did not want to purge because she had worked so hard in her recovery. However, the urge to rid herself of the large amount of food in her stomach was strong. She went into the bathroom and almost instinctively threw up. That is when she called me. We used the CBT cycle to explore the reasons for her relapse. The trig-

gering event was her "pig out" with her friends. Her
thoughts about that event were "I am going to gain 100
pounds and people will think I am fat." This led to her
feelings of fear and her feelings of fear led to her purging
behavior.

In my office, we challenged her non-productive
thoughts. She was able to identify the fact that overeating
at one meal is not going to cause her tremendous weight
gain, certainly not 100 pounds. In addition, she agreed
that it was highly improbable that due to this one meal,
people would think she was fat. Her shift in cognition
relieved her emotional distress. If she was able to do this
at the restaurant, she probably would not have engaged in
the ED behavior. Part of CBT is helping the person learn
how to be their own therapist. This requires giving them
the tools that they need to utilize when you are not with
them. Below we will talk about how insight-oriented work
in combination with CBT can be extremely helpful.

The other point of intervention when utilizing CBT is
behavioral. Behavioral changes are often easier to make
than cognitive changes. Therefore, therapists often start
with them and then move to examining unproductive cognitions. This is usually the order that I choose because
many of my patients do not have the tools necessary to
create change on their own. I want to give them these
tools early on and then work on the deeper cognitive
process later.

In order to create behavioral change, the person must
first identify the feeling(s) that lead to the ED behavior.
Without knowledge of why the person is engaging in the

ED behavior, they are not as likely to make a shift successfully. I strongly believe that restricting, binging, purging,
and over-exercising are coping mechanisms. It is a way for
the person with an ED to manage uncomfortable, distressing feelings that seem unmanageable. Therefore,
every treatment plan should include an exploration of
alternative behaviors. Increasing the individual's coping
mechanisms can ultimately lead to a decrease in the ED
behavior.

There are several steps necessary for success. First, you
must figure out the reason (Why?) behind the ED
behavior. For example, "I purge to relieve tension" (this is
a feeling state). Second, you must validate to the person
that the ED behavior is fulfilling a specific need. For
example, "You purge because it relieves tension and stress
and makes you feel better." Third, you can then explore
with the person what behaviors could potentially fulfill
that same need. For example, "What else could you do to
relieve tension and stress and feel better?" It is highly
important for the substitute/alternative behavior to fulfill
the same need. If it does not fulfill the same need, the
individual will be left feeling uncomfortable and in distress
and will continue to have the urge to restrict/binge/
purge.

I usually make a list of at least five alternative behaviors
with my patients. Finding these is generally a process
of trial and error. Some behaviors work and some do not.
Many of my patients do not know what will work until
they try out the different options. The goal is to give the
person alternative behaviors when they are feeling the

urge to restrict/binge/purge. Many individuals believe that their only option is to engage in these ED behaviors. For some it is habit forming and even addictive. It is the therapist's job to help them understand and create an alternative set of behaviors.

In the beginning, alternative behaviors may not provide the same relief that the eating disorder does. However, they will provide a way to experience genuine emotion, for better or for worse, which the individual needs to experience. It is through this process that the ED patient begins to learn how to cope in more positive and healthy ways. For an outline of this CBT process, please refer to Appendix A in the back of the book.

INSIGHT-ORIENTED THERAPY

In the process of utilizing CBT, I also employ insight-oriented therapy. Insight-oriented therapy uses talk therapy to discover and process unconscious thoughts and desires. This type of insight work helps the patient discover why they may have developed the eating disorder in the first place. With this understanding in place, they are better able to identify triggers and prevent relapse. They are also better able to figure why they are having certain thoughts about events that lead to the ED behavior. To illustrate this, let's go back to the example above, where the girl "pigged out" at the Mexican restaurant with her friends. The CBT interventions helped her to shift her cognitions. With a change in her thinking, she will experience a change in her feelings and then in her behavior. Although these changes are extremely important, because the goal is to stop the bulimic cycle from occurring, the underlining reason for her unproductive cognitive process is not addressed. Insight-oriented therapy can help accomplish this. Here is how it works:

First, the girl must identify her thoughts. Remember she stated that she was thinking, "I am going to gain 100 pounds and people will think I am fat." With CBT alone, the therapist would help the girl challenge these thoughts and then move on to shifting her behaviors. However, with insight-oriented work, the therapist would ask her to explore why she is having these thoughts in the first place. When working with this patient, I did just that. I told her that many people have "pigged out" at restaurants, but did not think what she was thinking. I validated to her that her thought process was not good or bad, right or wrong, but that she had it for a reason and we needed to find out what that reason was and where it came from. I often tell patients they are not born thinking this way. They do not pop out of the womb worrying about eating too much, gaining weight, and looking fat. It comes from somewhere. If willing, I take the patient through a process of discovery.

I asked this girl to think about what meaning she places on weight gain. Obviously, she is worried about gaining weight and looking fat. I asked her to think about what it would say about her as a person if she was overweight. She responded, "If I am fat, then I won't be popular." I dug a little deeper and said, "O.K., but a lot of people are not popular and they are okay with that. You clearly are not. This is not right or wrong, good or bad, but it is meaningful to you to be popular. Why? What would it say about you if you were not popular?" She responded, "If I am not popular, then people will not like me and I won't have any friends." I said to her, "A lot of people do not have many friends and they are okay with that. You are not. Why? What would it say about you if you had no friends?" She responded, "If I had no friends, I would be alone." I followed the same line of self-discovery and commented, "A lot of people like being alone. In fact, some prefer it." Then I asked her, "Why would being alone be upsetting to you? What meaning do you place on being alone?" After thinking for a moment, she responded, "If I am alone, then it means nobody likes me."

Her eyes filled with tears and she began to cry. Picking up on the pattern of dialogue, without my prompting she then said, "And if nobody likes me, then it means I am a loser. And if I am a loser then it means I am worthless." Further exploration of her thoughts led to a long discussion of her often thinking she is a disappointment to others. She does not feel "good enough" in sports, academically, or socially. These are what I call 'emotional truths.' These are not real truths per se, but very true feelings that a person experiences on a daily basis.

Obtaining this type of insight allows therapists to work with their patients at a deeper level. However, surface work is not superficial. It is very real and very important to the patient. CBT is one of the best ways to intervene at this level because it deals with the here and now and helps the patient make immediate changes. However, even though surface work is very important, deeper, insight-oriented work can bring about permanent change and prevent symptom jumping. Symptom jumping is when the person recovers from one problem such as an ED, but then jumps to a new problem such as substance abuse or self-mutilation.

It is not uncommon for individuals with eating disorders to symptom jump between AN and BN, especially during the recovery phase of treatment. In my experience, this happens primarily when someone diagnosed with AN begins to recover from the illness, but develops BN in the process. If this seems hard to imagine, consider this scenario. The anorexic individual must gain weight as part of their treatment plan. The process of gaining weight makes them feel miserable. They see themselves as fat, ugly and useless. In addition, their ability to be in control of something in their life (their weight) is now lost. They are petrified of gaining weight and yet unable to stop it.

The weight gain is partly due to the fact that they are being monitored by their doctor, nutritionist, and parents, and partly because their body will no longer cooperate. (This often happens in recovery to someone who is AN. They had no problem restricting earlier, but now they find it incredibly difficult. They report no longer having the willpower to restrict, and experiencing strong cravings for food. The latter sensation is similar to a person who has been on a diet, but craves food even more in the end and gains all the weight back.) In any case, they do not like the way they look or feel in their new body shape and size, and they engage in compensatory methods to deal with this distress. They hope to, at minimum, not gain any further weight, and ideally, to lose some weight as well. This compensatory method(s) becomes routine, and the bulimic cycle begins.

If symptom jumping occurs, CBT can be a useful intervention. Alternative behaviors and a shift in cognition can halt the cycle. Spending time understanding why the symptom jumping may be occurring can be accomplished through insight-oriented work. Whether the goal is to understand the onset of the eating disorder, the maintenance of the problem, symptom jumping, or relapse, insight-oriented work enables the patient to recognize the meaning behind her thoughts, feelings and behaviors. There are several treatment topics that therapists use in order to help the patient gain insight into her problem. For a detailed list of some of them, please see Appendix A.

I believe that when CBT and insight-oriented therapy are combined, the individual struggling with an ED has a greater chance of overcoming her illness. Accordingly, I blend the two approaches together to create a solid treatment plan for a person in individual therapy. To illustrate this, I would like to share with you the story below.

LISA'S STORY

Lisa is a 17-year-old girl who entered therapy after her 16th birthday. Lisa was resistant at first to seeing a psychologist. She was referred for sudden weight loss, but did not believe she had a problem. As a child she was always on "the chubby side," and was accustomed to hearing negative comments about her weight from coaches, family, and friends. Lisa was always a perfectionist. Even as young as three, her parents recall her intense frustration when she could not accomplish a task quickly and easily. In middle school, Lisa decided to go on a diet because she was tired of looking "less than perfect." All of her friends were "stick skinny" and she wasn't. She had a vision of what her ideal body should be and was determined to reach this goal. She began going to the gym to work out every morning before school for two hours and running track after school. She set up a meal plan that consisted of 1200 calories per day with little or no fat in her diet. This structured plan worked well during her eighth grade year and she lost ten pounds. She recalls looking better and feeling better at that time. The compliments she received from others about her willpower, drive, and appearance boosted her self-esteem immensely.

Lisa started high school with the same plan in place. However, upon entering high school something shifted. In middle school, everything always seemed to fall into place for her. People perceived her as smart, pretty, funny, and outgoing. In high school, she struggled with the work load, the social scene, and the friendships she made. She had not anticipated these struggles and was thrown off balance. She felt overwhelmed and increasingly inse-cure. She coped with these feelings by isolating herself, and by the time she entered her sophomore year, she had only one friend left. Alone almost all the time, she found comfort and security in going to school, studying, and working out at the gym.

Lisa's parents recognized her struggles and decided to surprise her with a trip to Europe to visit her cousins. She would spend the whole summer overseas before returning back to school in the fall. They thought it would be a nice break before she entered her junior year. Lisa was excited to go. Before she left, she was eating a healthy diet, and had a normal body weight.

When she returned three months later, she weighed 38 pounds less. Her hair was falling out, she appeared pale and malnourished, and she had stopped menstruating. She was so emaciated that she could not sit in a chair comfortably because her bones protruded from her skin.

Lisa's parents were shocked. They immediately sought help for her. She began attending individual therapy. Lisa talked about her trip to Europe in counseling. It was NOT everything she had hoped for. She got into a fight with her cousin the second week she was there, which left them not speaking to one another for the rest of the summer. Without her cousin's companionship, Lisa felt incredibly alone in a foreign country. To make matters worse, she had her first sexual experience while in Amsterdam, and it had not been consensual.

Lisa was in a pub (you are permitted at age 16 in Europe) with a 20-year-old foreigner who befriended her following the fight with her cousin. He bought her several drinks and asked her to come to his home. Feeling she had nowhere else to go, Lisa, who was intoxicated at the time, went with him. Once at his home, he started taking her clothes off. She protested vehemently and repeatedly, but he put her on his bed and had sex with her anyway.

Lisa described the experience as "dirty and unpleasant." After the sexual experience, he left the room and never came back. She stayed in his room, not knowing what to do. Early the next morning she got up to leave and found his family sitting around the breakfast table looking at her "strangely." She was incredibly embarrassed and ashamed.

Lisa got herself back to her cousin's house and spent the next several days alone in her room, beating herself up mentally and physically for making such a "bad choice." She blamed herself and hit herself physically as punishment for getting in to such a stupid situation. She could not eat or sleep. She became very depressed. When she missed her menstrual cycle a few weeks later, she was certain she was pregnant. Lisa remembers thinking if she were to starve herself, maybe the baby would not get the nutrients it needed and she would miscarry. This is when she stopped eating completely.

It was not until Lisa started talking about her traumatic experience in Amsterdam that she realized she had been sexually assaulted. She was blaming herself for a poor choice, when in fact, she had been raped. The perpetrator got her drunk and then did not stop his sexual advances when Lisa asked him to, which clearly makes the experience nonconsensual and forcible under the statutes of the law.

Lisa's Treatment

Lisa chose to engage in individual therapy. In setting up a treatment plan with Lisa, a nutritionist and medical doctor were brought in to aid in her treatment. Therapy focused on working through the traumatic experience and removing her intense, overwhelming feelings of self-blame. She experienced unproductive thoughts constantly that led to her feelings of guilt. CBT helped her to change her cognitions and relieve her distressing emotions. Lisa was able to make the connection between the rape and her decline into an eating disorder, with her long history of body weight issues. Insight-oriented therapy helped her to accomplish this.

There are many common precipitating factors that lead to AN. For Lisa, one factor was her failure to develop mastery or control over herself and the world around her. Lisa was able to recognize that she always wanted to be thin and beautiful and to have control over her weight. For the first time, she felt like she was able to achieve this goal. She felt if she was not thin, she was neither beautiful nor loveable. Her mentality was "all or nothing," with no middle ground. The trauma she faced on her overseas trip pushed her more quickly into a desire for starvation. Dieting became an isolated area of personal control for her.

Another factor was Lisa's lack of awareness of bodily processes, and the feelings that accompanied the changes in her own body and shape. She reported during one therapy session that she was always afraid to grow up and become a woman. It is worth noting that she went on her first diet around the same time that she began puberty. She was very unhappy about developing breasts and beginning menstruation. Rebelling against the outward signs of womanhood, Lisa refused to wear a bra. She did not perceive the changes her body was going through as natural. Like many individuals with AN, Lisa viewed her body as something foreign that must be artificially controlled through weight loss.

In addition, Lisa had deficits in her self-esteem and self-regulation, both precipitating factors in her diagnosis of AN. These deficits left her feeling unprepared for the developmental task of separation and individuation. She talked a lot in therapy about her fear of going away to college and being out on her own. Her relationship with her mother was extremely close, with enmeshed boundaries that made the idea of separating scary and challenging for her.

Lisa's way of thinking was also a precipitating factor to her eating disorder. As noted earlier, she sees things as black or white with no gray areas. This thinking style is common among individuals with AN. Lisa sees herself as fat or thin, beautiful or ugly, smart or stupid. There are no "in betweens," which can be very discouraging. Performance and achievement are tied into this thinking style as well, in that the individual sees herself either as highly successful or as a complete failure. Interestingly, Lisa's performance and achievements are tied more to pleasing others than to pleasing herself. This is also very common among people with AN, which makes them particularly vulnerable to influences of culture, family, and peer groups.

Lisa's family dynamics also reflect some of these precipitating factors. Her mother presented with genuine concern for her daughter. Her father was concerned but uncomfortable with psychological treatment. He stated openly that he did not believe in therapy. Lisa described her relationship with her mother as extremely close, and noted that her mother was her best friend. She viewed her relationship with her father, however, as strained due to his "control over her life." However, Lisa excused his need to control everyone around him, stating that it was due to his cultural upbringing. She noted that all of her family in Europe were very controlling and "that's just the way they are." Lisa's relationship with her brother was almost non-existent since they rarely saw each other due to conflicting schedules.

Lisa's parents had some tension in their marriage, which increased when Lisa's eating disorder placed additional stress on the family. During the intake session, the family noted their concern about the length and the cost of treatment. The parents expressed interest in a fast solution to the problem. This angered Lisa who found their concern over money and time a great insult. She pointed out that the family had plenty of money and that her eating problems have been longstanding and might take time to resolve. She stated that she hoped she was a priority to them.

All of the precipitating factors to AN mentioned have their roots in the individual and the individual's relationships to others. However, the importance of societal influences cannot be dismissed, particularly in the United States, where so much emphasis is placed on being thin and beautiful. As we have already discussed, in some circumstances, societal influences can act as a precipitating factor to an ED, and in almost all cases, can exacerbate and prolong the symptoms of the disorder. This was particularly true in Lisa's case. Her peer group strives to be thin and beautiful because that is what they believe will make them popular, and this, along with her family's focus on success and achievement, has had a great influence on her. Lisa's desire to be thin, and her belief that being thin would bring her happiness, were challenged constantly during the course of treatment through CBT.

Lisa placed particular emphasis on the influence of advertisements and the media. She noted that she has been obsessed for as long as she can remember with looking at magazines, and comparing her perceived body image with her ideal body image. Basing an ideal body image on models from a magazine can be discouraging and dangerous. Lisa has not thrown any of her magazines away so that she can go back and see how close she is getting to her ideal. She has stacks of magazines in her garage to refer to.

Given Lisa's intense focus on body image, much of her treatment has been spent assessing and lessening her degree of body dissatisfaction. Lisa has begun to learn to accept her body and feel more comfortable with it (CBT). This is significant given the trauma she faced and her resultant feelings of dirtiness and damage. Since the trauma was her first and only sexual experience, it has left her with intense fears about sex and her own sexuality. The meaning of the sexual experience has also caused difficulties for her in that "having sex means becoming a woman." This is something Lisa has been fighting against due to her fears of separation and individuation. Recognizing the sexual experience as a rape seemed to lessen her fears about "growing up" (Insight-Oriented Therapy).

It may even be possible that Lisa unconsciously placed herself in a high-risk situation as an attempt at individuation, not realizing that a traumatic event would ensue. If this is true, then she would perceive this attempt as a failure, which in turn could have caused the desire for her to return to her childhood. The ultimate regression may be AN since we know individuals with this illness take on the traits of a much younger person (no menses, etc.)

Lisa's treatment plan included weekly individual therapy sessions and regular appointments with her nutritionist and medical doctor. She remained in treatment for one full year and was able to regain the weight she lost. She still struggles with body image and self-esteem. However, she has learned to better accept who she is as person and not focus her identity solely on her appearance. CBT has helped Lisa change her thinking style. She is better able to see gray areas and not think in extremes. Furthermore, she was able to discard many of her unproductive cognitions about herself and her accomplishments. She began working toward goals for herself instead of for others, which has helped her to feel pride in her achievements. Unfortunately, however, treatment was not completed with full success. Lisa terminated treatment after one year per her parent's request. The family did not want to spend the money to keep her in therapy any longer.

From the beginning, the family resisted participating in Lisa's treatment even though family therapy was recommended. As noted above, Lisa made some wonderful progress in many areas, however, her eating disorder changed from AN to BN very quickly upon termination of treatment (symptom jumping). Her parents refused to place her back in therapy due to the cost and their feelings that she was not trying hard enough to make a change. They were disappointed with her lack of motivation to get well. The family continues to resist family treatment.

Family therapy is one of the most successful types of treatment for eating disorders, when the patient is an adolescent. However, this type of treatment can also be extremely helpful when the patient is a young adult. For Lisa, the family dynamics are very much a part of the problem. If Lisa's family participated in therapy, I believe they might also achieve a greater understanding of the problem and find creative solutions to support her recovery.

7

FAMILY THERAPY

INTRODUCTION

As in the case of individual therapy, there are many different types of family therapy utilized in treating eating disorders. While it is impossible to go over all of them, I will share a type of therapy that is gaining popularity due to its high effectiveness rates. I was lucky to have the opportunity to be trained in this type of therapy several years ago by Dr. James Lock at Stanford University, School of Medicine in the Psychiatry Department. I have been using this method ever since. It is a family therapy called the Maudsley Model, also known as the Maudsley Approach. This type of therapy was manualized in 2001 by four researchers, James Lock, Daniel LeGrange, W. Stewart Agras, and Christopher Dare. They published the manual for family therapy with anorexic patients. However, subsequent research had proven its effectiveness

with bulimic patients as well. (Treatment Manual for
Anorexia Nervosa, 2001). I use this approach for both AN
and BN in my practice.

FAMILY THERAPY: THE MAUDSLEY APPROACH

The Maudsley Approach recognizes that, without
proper intervention, eating disorders will most
likely become a chronic problem involving multiple hospi-
talizations and prolonged treatment. Therefore, it is specifically designed to intervene aggressively in the early
stages of the illness. It is based on a short term therapy
model, so treatment is often only 20 sessions over a six-
month period. It is best utilized by families where the
eating-disordered family member is under the age of
18 and still living at home. The reason for this is that the
family is seen as one of the greatest resources for change.
This approach focuses on the strengths of the family and
their creative resources to move their child toward
recovery. In doing so, it also exonerates parents from
blame.

The primary tenet of the Maudsley approach, which at
first was solely used with individuals diagnosed with
AN, is that the adolescent is embedded in the family, and
that the parents' involvement in therapy is crucial for success in treatment. In addition, the adolescent
with the AN is viewed as not capable of making rational
decisions about food and weight as long as her self-starvation remains active. Therefore, parents should be in
charge of re-feeding their child, while showing respect and
regard for the adolescent's point of view and experience.

Accordingly, parents are temporarily asked to take responsibility for food and weight issues to help reduce the hold this disorder has over the adolescent's life. Once successful in this task, parents return appropriate control to the adolescent and assist her in the negotiation of predictable adolescent development tasks. Thus, in relation to eating only, the adolescent is seen as not functioning on an adolescent level, but instead as a much younger child who is in need of a great deal of help from her parents. In addition, the Maudsley approach focuses therapeutic attention on the task of weight restoration, particularly in the early stages of treatment.

In the case of BN, the primary focus is not that much different. However, instead of working toward weight restoration, which is usually not necessary with the bulimic individual, the family works toward finding a balance between eating enough food to be healthy and medically safe, and avoiding compensatory methods following food consumption. In other words, the family must help the eating disordered family member find a balance so that the urge to binge and then purge/fast/over-exercise is diminished. As with AN, parents are temporarily asked to take responsibility for food and weight issues, and to monitor for compensatory methods. Once successful in this task, parents return appropriate control to the adolescent and support her as necessary in ordinary adolescent issues.

The Maudsley approach to family therapy has three clearly defined phases. In the first phase, the focus is on correcting severe malnutrition associated with AN by having parents take charge of feeding their son or daughter. If the individual is purging, fasting or over-exercising, it is in this phase that the parents identify and disallow this activity. Therapy aims to establish and reinforce a strong parental alliance around re-feeding their offspring, while also attempting to align the patient with the sibling sub-system. This phase also includes a family meal that allows the therapist to observe familial interaction patterns around eating. The therapist stresses that parents did not cause the illness while also demonstrating how the ED has dramatically changed their child's behavior . These observations highlight the differences between eating-disordered thinking and the patient's former concerns, and clearly separate the disorder from the patient. When the patient accepts the demands of the parents and steady weight gain is evident, and/or purging/fasting/over-exercising behaviors are extinct, the second phase begins.

This phase encourages parents to help their child take more control over eating under their supervision. Whether it is eating more, as is in the case for the anorexic individual, or eating normally without binging and then engaging in compensatory methods, the goal is for the person to be more responsible for their own meals again. When this is accomplished, and the patient's weight has stabilized at near 95% of ideal body weight without significant parental supervision and without the use of compensatory methods, then the third phase begins.

The third phase of treatment begins to focus on the impact the ED has had upon establishing a healthy adolescent identity. This entails a review of central issues of adolescence e.g., supporting increased personal autonomy for the adolescent, familial boundary management, and supporting parental focus on their life as a couple.

BRENDA'S STORY

Brenda is 16 years old. She is a Caucasian female who was referred by her physician after being diagnosed with Anorexia Nervosa, Binge-Eating/ Purging Type. Her physician had a difficult time diagnosing her because her behavior also fit the symptoms of Bulimia Nervosa. Her binges were not small or even medium-sized meals that she would purge afterwards. They were very large binges that fit the criteria for BN. However, given her significant weight loss in a very short period of time as well as her intense fear of weight gain, her doctor confirmed a diagnosis of AN with the subtype of binge/purge.

Brenda is 5'8" tall with an ideal body weight of 140 pounds. Prior to her referral, Brenda lost 35 pounds within a six-month period. This severe weight loss caused her to become medically unstable. Her temperature was low and her heart rate was irregular, placing her at risk for cardiac arrhythmia and/or congestive heart failure. She was hospitalized weighing 104 pounds. Brenda remained in the hospital for two weeks where she slowly gained weight. When she was discharge from the hospital she weighed 111 pounds. It was at this time that she was referred for family treatment.

Brenda lives at home with her immediate family, which includes her parents, John and Judy, and her older brother, Tom. Her father runs their family business and Tom works by his side every day. Her father and brother are very close. They are always together and Brenda often feels left out. She would like to have a better relationship with both of them, especially her brother whom she looks up to and admires. Brenda does feel connected and close to her mother. Brenda's mother used to help out in the family business; however, she stopped when Brenda began struggling with her eating disorder. Judy wanted to give her daughter her full attention and was committed to helping her overcome her problem. Unfortunately, she was not successful and Brenda ended up in the hospital.

Prior to the onset of the illness, Brenda described herself as outgoing and happy. Now she describes herself as "a sad and confused person living in an overwhelming world." She remembers when life was simple. She went to school and got good grades, she spent time with her many friends as well as her boyfriend, and she worked out daily with her sports team. This all changed with when something tragic happened in her family.

One year ago her paternal grandmother, with whom she was very close, passed away. The death was a surprise; although the family was concerned that she was sick, they did not think her life was in danger. She had developed kidney stones and was being treated at a treatment center located near their home. She went into septic shock from the treatment, which led to her sudden death. Brenda was devastated. She could not understand how something like this could happen. One minute her grandmother was there and the next minute she was gone. She felt completely out of control and immediately began searching for ways to numb her pain.

Some of Brenda's friends smoked marijuana and talked about how relaxed it made them feel. Brenda was willing to try anything to "relax" and escape the reality of her grandmother's death. She began smoking a few times a month and then more frequently to get the same effect. Although she liked the way it made her feel in the moment, there was a particular consequence of smoking pot that she did not like. She started gaining weight. Every time she smoked, she ate extraordinary amounts of food (known as "the munchies"). She did not find this sudden weight gain attractive and wanted to do something about it. She was not exercising regularly anymore. After her grandmother died, she could not bring herself to go to practice. Her team dropped her for not showing up. This gave her more time to smoke pot and hang around the house, which led to even more opportunities to eat and gain weight.

Brenda wanted to compensate for her weight gain, and at the same time, still numb her emotions. She started taking methamphetamines. She abused methamphetamines with friends on a weekly basis during that time period. She says she began using them as a way to lose weight, get high, and escape her sadness all at the same time. She stopped using these drugs when her friends stopped because she no longer had free access to them. Luckily, she was not dependent on them and quit rather easily. However, she did what I have already referenced in this book - she symptom jumped. Instead of engaging in substance abuse, she began engaging in eating disorder behaviors. When she stopped using drugs, she began purging. After every "munchi-binge", she purged. It became a habit. She liked the way it felt to get rid of the food she had just eaten. She said it was a way for her to feel in control after an out-of-control binge.

Brenda began losing weight and started to receive compliments from friends and family. Her boyfriend gave her the most praise. She liked pleasing others, and it did not take long for her to make the connection between losing weight and feeling good about herself. She stopped smoking pot because she did not want to crave food. She began restricting and purging up to six times per day. She was consumed with thoughts of food, calories and body image. She couldn't concentrate in school because her mind was filled with eating-disordered thoughts. She failed her classes and began independent study. She was still off her team and getting no exercise. She reported not sleeping well and feeling incredibly irritable and depressed most of the time. She avoided her friends because she "liked being alone when eating and definitely when throwing up." She did spend time with her boyfriend, but even that did was not the same and she often wished she could be alone.

Brenda's friends recognized that there was a problem and contacted Brenda's mother to inform her of their concerns. Her parents also recognized that there was a problem and began to identify the signs and symptoms of an eating disorder. Judy and John decided to take her to see a therapist. Brenda met with the therapist for close to one year but did not make much progress. She continued to engage in restricting, binging and purging behaviors. Her parents began to feel incredibly helpless and hopeless. They tried to express their thoughts to their daughter, but she shut them down. She would not talk about her problem with them and basically stopped to talking to them altogether. She would not eat with them, go on family outings with them or even remain in the same room with them when they were home. Her symptoms worsened, and that is what brought her to the hospital.

Brenda was hospitalized for malnutrition secondary to AN. When she entered the hospital, not only was she malnourished, but her hair was falling out and she had developed lanugo on her legs and arms. In addition, she had tooth decay, electrolyte imbalance, sore throats, constipation, dehydration, dizziness, low energy, low temperature, low blood pressure, and bradycardia. She did not think things would go this far. The hospital was definitely a wake-up call for her. It was the first time in a long time that she found some motivation to change. She thought about how sad her grandmother would be if she were alive to see her in this place in her life. She made a promise to herself and to her grandmother to work toward recovery.

Brenda's Treatment

Brenda and her family entered family therapy using the Maudsley Model. This treatment approach utilizes many different interventions from a variety of theoretical approaches. In many ways it is psychodynamic in nature. The therapist makes interpretations all the time; however, they are not shared openly with the family members. Instead they are used to guide the therapist in the selection of other techniques. In Brenda's case, I strongly believe that she began developing her eating disorder due to her fear of growing up. She was hit with two realities at the same time; that some things are completely out of one's control and that, as one gets older, one's responsibilities greatly increase.

Two significant events occurred at the onset of Brenda's illness. We already talked about the first one. Brenda's grandmother died suddenly leaving her feeling devastated, shocked, and confused. The death of her grandmother was completely out of her control. It was out of everyone's control. She did not even have a chance to say goodbye. Right around the same time, her brother, Tom, graduated from high school and moved out of the house. Following these two incidents, Brenda began to develop eating disorder symptoms.

In both of these circumstances, Brenda experienced a great loss. She experienced a loss when her grandmother died as well as a loss with her brother's departure from the home; however, it was his sudden return that I believe affected her more. After attempting to live independently for three months, Tom was forced to move back in with his family because he could not support himself financially even with a full-time job. The reality of life and death and the responsibilities that come with adulthood may have caused intrapsychic conflicts for Brenda around issues of separation and individuation. Intrapsychic is a psychological term referring to internal psychological processes.

In the prevention chapter, we talked about some of the theories regarding the development of an eating disorder. Some theorists believe the development of AN, (which was Brenda's formal diagnosis), is the ultimate regression to dependency and is caused by the individual's fear of growing up and becoming a woman. Therefore, the individual with AN prevents physical maturation through self-starvation. Physically, the individual with AN loses a severe amount a weight. As her body size decreases, she appears smaller and much younger looking than her actual age. Furthermore, the individual with AN stops menstruating. Brenda stopped menstruating for four months. The change in physical appearance along with becoming amenorrheic provides the individual with a way to remain in a child's body avoiding the responsibilities and demands of adulthood. This may be exactly what triggered this illness with Brenda given the significant events in her life that led up to the onset of her eating disorder.

COURSE OF THERAPY

Brenda's family entered a twelve-month treatment program, which provided them with 20 sessions throughout the course of a year. The first seven sessions were weekly, the next seven were every other week and the remaining six were monthly. All sessions were 50-60 minutes in duration, except for the family meal, which took approximately 90 minutes. The first ten minutes of each session was spent individually with Brenda. During this time, Brenda was weighed and had the opportunity to bring up any issues or concerns before entering the family session.

Initially, Brenda's family had ambivalent feelings toward the Maudsley approach. On the one hand, they were all clearly motivated to help Brenda. On the other hand, they all felt somewhat hopeless that any changes would occur. After all, Judy had quit working to support her daughter and even that had not helped. In addition, they already had her in individual therapy and that had not helped either. Clearly they were somewhat skeptical that this type of intervention would create some change.

Brenda's parents were very caring, but frustrated with their daughter's "unwillingness to eat and get well." Brenda's brother was distant from his sister and unsure of his role in the family treatment. He was quiet and withdrawn in the beginning of therapy, withholding important insights and observations about the family structure and process. Brenda was anxious and introverted. She, too, initially withheld important insights and information regarding her family during early family sessions. However, prior to the start of the family treatment, she did share some of her insights in private. For example, Brenda commented that she did not think family therapy would work because her family did not communicate well with one another. She was willing to give the treatment a try, but predicted that she would be blamed and scapegoated for all the family problems during the course of therapy.

At the beginning of treatment, the family structure was hierarchical. This means that John and Judy represented the executive subsystem and were very much in control of all the family decisions. John was viewed by all family members as the "head of the household" with a domineering presence. Judy was viewed as the supportive caretaker who followed the lead of her husband. She was also seen as the "peacemaker" of the family. When conflicts arose, it was her job to facilitate and encourage resolution. Tom held the role of the stereotypical older brother. He was protective of his sister, but was easily annoyed by her and spent little time with her.

Initially, all the family members were very disappointed with Brenda for her lack of effort in overcoming her eating disorder. Brenda clearly needed all family members to help her fight against her illness and was receiving little assistance in this task. Her mother thought she was helping and tried her best, but many of the things she did actually caused Brenda to feel blamed and criticized and then in turn to restrict or binge and purge. Brenda and Tom were clearly disconnected and distant from one another, which provided no basis for a strong sibling support system. Furthermore, Brenda's relationship with her parents was clearly strained. Her relationship with her father was not close and her relationship with her mother worsened with the onset of her eating disorder. Brenda desperately needed her parent's support and was constantly worried that instead she would receive criticism and blame for causing the problems in the family.

As mentioned above, the course of family therapy based on the Maudsley model involves consistent family participation throughout three phases of treatment. The first phase focuses on re-feeding the anorexic patient and avoiding compensatory methods of weight loss while focusing on the eating disorder symptoms. In this phase, attempts are made to empower the parental system to creatively proceed with this task and to align the anorexic patient with her sibling(s) for support. Throughout this phase of treatment, the therapist facilitates discussion and provides the client with empathy for her predicament of needing to be re-fed in order to survive, and the feeling that her parents are "taking away" her only sense of self.

During the first session, the therapist sets the tone for the entire first phase of treatment. Therefore, this session is incredibly important and must be handled well in order to reinforce the importance of full family participation. There are three main goals for session one: (1) to engage the family in the therapy, (2) to obtain a history of how the AN is affecting the family, and (3) to obtain preliminary information about how the family functions (i.e. coalitions, authority structure, conflicts, etc.).

At the end of session one, the therapist asks the parents to bring a family meal to the second session. The parents are instructed to bring a meal for the anorexic family member that will nurse her back to health. In other words, a meal that meets the nutritional requirements to help with their daughter's starved state. There are three main goals for this session: (1) to continue the assessment of the family structure and its likely impact on the ability of the parents to successfully re-feed their daughter, (2) to provide an opportunity for the parents to experience success in re-feeding their daughter, and (3) to assess the family process specifically during eating.

The remainder of phase I is characterized by the therapist's attempts to bring the patient's food intake under parental control. This is done by expanding, reinforcing, and repeating some of the tasks initiated at the beginning of therapy. The therapist not only has to continue the work done in sessions one and two, but must also regularly discuss with the parents their attempts at re-feeding their daughter and systematically advise them on how to proceed in curtailing the influence of the eating disorder. These sessions can be viewed as repetitious, but are extremely necessary in order to facilitate parental consistency in the management of their child's illness. The unrelenting focus on weight gain and health during the first phase sets the Maudsley treatment apart from other family approaches. There are three main goals for the remainder of treatment sessions in phase I: (1) to keep the family focused on the eating disorder, (2) to help the parents take charge of their daughters eating, and (3) to mobilize siblings to support the patient in recovery.

Brenda's family was highly critical of Brenda (as she predicted) during the first phase of treatment. A significant portion of these early sessions was focused on attempting to decrease these family criticisms by helping the family to understand how little control over her behavior Brenda actually had. The first session's focus on the dire outcomes of chronic AN raised enough anxiety in

the family to motivate the parents to try once again to help
Brenda. Much of the first session focused on reinforcing
for the family that they were the greatest resource for
recovery that Brenda had, and that she would need all of
their support in order to be successful in the fight against
her illness. Because Brenda's family had been excluded
from her treatment in the past, they were grateful to be
included at this time.

The family strengths of caring, commitment, and support for Brenda against her illness were the focus in session 1. At first, Brenda's family struggled with the idea of
seeing the illness as something separate from Brenda, but
in subsequent sessions they increasingly understood the
important distinction between fighting against the illness
and fighting against their daughter. Brenda was able to tell
her parents in the first session that their criticism and
blame of her made things worse for her and caused her to
want to restrict her intake as well as binge and purge more
frequently. Brenda's family was able to hear this and
promised to try to decrease their critical and statements.

Session 2, which is the family meal, helped the family
members clarify their roles in the fight against the ED.
Brenda's parents did a good job of getting Brenda to eat
more than she intended to, while at the same time not
allowing her to eat too much which would inevitably lead
to a purge. At times the family became critical once again
of Brenda's resistance to eating. However, during these
times, I was able to role model non-critical ways to intervene with Brenda and encourage her to increase her food
intake. Tom seemed especially relieved that he did not

have to be in charge of Brenda's eating. This had caused several arguments with his sister in the past. He appreciated his parents' role in re-feeding and easily adjusted to his role of supporting his sister. He made several positive comments to his sister and lent her support when she did not want to eat anymore. For example, Tom told her that he knew eating was hard for her and recognized that she was probably feeling really full after eating. Therefore, when the meal was finished he was willing to go on a long walk with her before they drove home so she could digest some of her food and not feel so full.

Subsequent to session 2, due to Brenda's eating disorder difficulties, she was unable to attend school and remain safe. Her parents recognized the need to monitor her food consumption and her purging behaviors. Therefore, the family decided that Brenda should stay at home and participate in independent study while she recovered from her illness. This decision was implemented at the beginning of phase I and was carried out during the entire course of treatment.

During the first phase of treatment, Brenda gradually began accepting her parent's efforts to monitor her food intake and purging behaviors. Thus the rest of phase I focused on what worked and what did not work for Brenda in the family's efforts to fight together against the illness. For example, Brenda noted that it was not helpful for her parents to stare at her during meal times and to count out all of the calories she was consuming. Instead, she wanted her mother to prepare a plate for her just like everyone else's (with normal proportions) and then monitor that she eventually ate everything on her plate. This helped Brenda in two important ways; it prevented food restriction and it prevented binge eating. In addition, following each meal, Brenda's mother or father would supervise her to ensure that no purging took place.

During one of the sessions in phase I, Brenda noted that although she understood why her parents needed to supervise her after each meal, it was not helpful when they stared at her and followed her all around the house. Instead, she requested that they monitor her whereabouts from where they were situated in the home. Brenda's parents agreed to this request. However, they believed it was necessary to have increased supervision during bathroom visits. As a result, an agreement was made that Brenda would leave the bathroom door open "just a crack" with a parent standing outside the door to monitor her actions. This allowed Brenda the privacy she wanted and gave her parents the security they needed to know whether or not she was engaging in any purging behaviors. Helping the family figure out what is effective and what is not effective in the re-feeding process is a very important part of phase I because it begins to prepare the adolescent to take over their own re-feeding in ways that work specifically for them.

As mentioned above, the second phase of treatment focuses on negotiations for a new pattern of relationships. It begins when the patient is able to accept the re-feeding process directed by the parents and a shift in mood among family members occurs. Eating disorder symptoms remain the focus of the treatment sessions, but the tension is clearly reduced during discussions about the necessity of weight gain. During the second phase, other discussion topics may be added into the treatment session that are related to the parents' difficult task of restoring their child's weight.

There are three main goals for phase II of treatment: (1) to maintain parental management of eating disorder symptoms until the patient shows evidence that she is able to eat well and gain weight independently, (2) to return food and weight control to the adolescent, and (3) to explore the relationship between adolescent developmental issues and the ED.

The beginning of phase II was marked by a shift in Brenda's overall mood and her ability to eat well on her own with little encouragement from her parents. Brenda was much less irritable, more outgoing, and visibly happier than at the start of treatment. In phase II, her energy level was higher and she was more talkative in sessions. She had increased confidence about what she was eating and how she looked; her body image was less distorted. Brenda noted that in the beginning of treatment she used to think about food 99% of her day and during phase II of treatment she only thought about food 40% of her day. Furthermore, during phase II, Brenda was purging approximately one time per week, which was greatly reduced from several times per day at the beginning of treatment.

Negotiations were held between Brenda and her parents to return the task of re-feeding to Brenda. This happened slowly and carefully. As Brenda's parents became more comfortable with her ability to eat on her own, they began to monitor her less frequently. For example, they allowed her to prepare her own meals at home and occasionally go out to dinner with her friends. With each success, Brenda was given more responsibility to monitor her own food intake as well as her urges to purge. Conversely with each setback, Brenda was given less responsibility and more support from her family to monitor the eating disorder symptoms.

Throughout these negotiations, Brenda's family was always available for reinforcement, encouragement, and support. Brenda often utilized her family's support during the second phase of treatment. For example, one night she went out to dinner with her boyfriend and became very full after the meal. She asked her boyfriend to take her home immediately so that she could talk to her mother. Her mother provided her with many encouraging statements and ideas of how to fight against the urge to purge. One suggestion was to go on a long walk to help digest the food while talking about all of her accomplishments in recovery so far. Brenda followed through with this suggestion and felt much better afterwards with no purging episodes.

As Brenda became more in control of re-feeding herself, other issues became apparent in the therapy. At the end of the second phase of treatment, connections were made between adolescent developmental issues and the ED. For example, Brenda often talked about her fear of growing up. She was able to make the connection between the development of her eating disorder and the recognition that some things are completely out of one's control, and that as one get older, one's responsibilities greatly increase. Her fears of growing up and having more responsibility were discussed. Brenda's parents helped to reinforce that, even though she was getting older and would be taking the responsibilities of adulthood, they would always be there to support her and help her in any way necessary. This reinforcement seemed to help a great deal by lessening Brenda's anxiety about the high expectations she had of becoming an adult. To support his sister during this discussion, Tom reminded Brenda of his own struggles with transitioning into adulthood and their parents' support of him when he needed it the most. After attempting to live independently for three months, Tom was forced to move back in with his family because he could not support himself financially even with a full time job. Judy and John welcomed him back into their home, and provided him with financial and emotional support.

As described earlier in the chapter, the third phase of treatment focuses on general adolescent development. It is initiated when the patient's weight is restored to health and self-starvation has ceased. This phase helps the family establish healthy interactions between parent and adolescent where the main focus of their interactions is not based on the eating disorder. Instead it is focused on issues such autonomy and individuation for the adolescent, and appropriate family boundaries.

During phase III, adolescent issues were addressed separately from the eating disorder. Issues such as dating, sex, substance use, college, and financial responsibilities were all discussed and processed in the context of the family therapy sessions. Brenda's parents attempted to use their problem-solving skills to process some of the more difficult issues in a positive, supportive way. However, at times, their criticisms re-emerged, leading to arguments and a breakdown of communication. During these times, the therapist intervened to remind the family of the negative consequences of critical comments on Brenda's recovery. For example, the topic of dating and sex was brought up many times during phase III due to the increasing amount of time Brenda was spending with her boyfriend. During one family session about this topic, Brenda's father commented that Brenda was too dependent on her boyfriend and that if she continued to be this way, she would never grow up and be able to take care of herself. Brenda was offended and became argumentative. The re-emergence of critical comments was delicately pointed out to the family by the therapist, which led to a dramatic shift in communication. The family discussed dating and sex in an open and non-judgmental manner.

It is important to note that phase III is relatively short and has a limited focus. While adolescent issues are important and can be the subject of family in and of themselves, they are not the priority of the Maudsley approach, which remains intently focused on overcoming the ED itself. Addressing adolescent issues is usually the primary focus of other types of family therapy and would customarily be a priority in helping an adolescent recover from an eating disorder. However, the Maudsley approach differs in that the therapist primarily focuses his/her attention on the task of weight restoration and avoidance of compensatory methods, and only focuses on adolescent issues when weight is stabilized and self-starvation/binging/purging/over-exercising has abated. However, focusing on adolescent issues apart from the eating disorder even to a limited degree was beneficial for the family, because this solidified the successes gained in Brenda's recovery. It also provided the family with a model of how to better communicate and solve problems at home.

Perhaps the most striking difference observed in the family during the third phase of treatment was the change in their family dynamics. As noted earlier, they entered treatment filled with frustration and anger, and very critical of one another. They were quick to blame each other, and had poor communication skills. The relationships between Brenda and her brother wer strained, as were the relationships between Brenda and her parents. By the time the family reached the third phase of treatment, their relationships were greatly improved.

For example, Tom went from telling his sister "You are such a spoiled brat. You eat all the food and then throw it up so there is nothing left for anyone else. I can't wait to move out of here," to telling his sister how much he cared about her and how much he loved her. Tom's task of providing his sister with support during the recovery process allowed him to help his sister get her mind off purging when she felt the urge. He took her to the beach, the movies, and on long walks until her urges passed.

Brenda's relationship with her parents also greatly improved. Initially, John and Judy struggled with separating the illness from Brenda, and blamed her for her lack of effort in eating. However, by the third phase of treatment, if discussion of the eating disorder came up at all, the parents were quick to state that the ED was to blame for their daughter getting ill and causing the problems in the family. With few signs and symptoms of the ED still present (some body image distortion), the family was able to focus on adolescent issues mentioned above.

Brenda's family remained in therapy for a full year. Her progress was gradual, and she gained weight steadily from the beginning of treatment when she weighed 111 pounds. Her lowest weight was 104 (prior to her hospitalization). At the end of family treatment, she weighed 131 pounds and had not engaged in any purging behavior for over three months. As described above, the family learned how to openly communicate with one another in non-critical ways. Their relationships were strengthened and they recognized that their support of one another led to their success in fighting against the ED and helping Brenda in her recovery.

CONCLUSION

As mentioned before, there are several different types of family therapy that are utilized by highly skilled experts in the field of mental health. The Maudsley Model is just one of them. However, its presentation here illustrates the many different types of approaches used by therapists when working with an eating disorder patient because the Maudsely Model incorporates many of them. It utilizes structural family therapy, strategic family therapy, narrative family therapy, and CBT interventions to bring about change in the eating disorder patient and their family system.

Since I had the privilege of working with James Lock, M.D. at Stanford Medical School of Medicine in the Psychiatry Department performing this type of treatment on families in the Bay Area, I saw firsthand the success that it brought to these individuals. I conducted my own research study to examine the outcome and effectiveness of the Maudsley Model on families with a member who was diagnosed with AN (A Descriptive Study of the Perceived Reasons for the Effectiveness of a Time Limited, Family Based Therapy Approach for Adolescents Diagnosed with Anorexia Nervosa, 2002; Patient Perspectives on Manualized Family Therapy for Adolescents with Anorexia Nervosa, 2001).

I had the opportunity to work with AN, restricting type as well as AN, purging type. I also had the opportunity to work with bulimic patients who symptom jumped during their course of recovery. Results from the above mentioned study indicated that a time-limited manualized family treatment based on the Maudsley Approach was acceptable to parents and patients with the disorder and with a specific focus on AN. For the most part, families reported high degrees of satisfaction with its effectiveness. On the other hand, a substantial minority felt that additional therapy, especially individual therapy was warranted. To date no study has combined individual and family therapy for AN to test its efficacy. Such a study would potentially add to our understanding of how best to treat ED's in adolescents.

8

Ending Treatment and Relapse Prevention

When your child's therapist informs you that she is ready to stop treatment, it is very important to inquire whether or not relapse prevention has been addressed in their sessions together. It is not uncommon for a child to relapse. Unfortunately, patients can fall into old traps and revert back to negative behaviors. The trick is to help the child learn to identify these traps and make choices before they feel like they are in crisis and have the urge to restrict/binge/purge/over-exercise. If the therapist is able to do this, the chances of relapse are greatly reduced. This is a very important part of treatment and, unfortunately, one that is often overlooked.

REASONS FOR RELAPSE

There are several possible reasons for relapse. One of the main reasons that people relapse is because of *secondary gains.* Secondary gains are indirect reasons for maintaining eating disorder behaviors. They are secondary to the primary reasons already discussed. For example, think about a child who, during the course of her eating disorder, received a lot of attention from her family. Prior to the eating disorder, she may not have received much attention at all. She was one of five children in the home, and both her parents worked full time jobs in order to support the family. Nannies were inconsistent, her older siblings wanted nothing to do with her, and her younger siblings were a pain so she avoided them. Although her eating disorder did not develop because of a lack of attention from family, the increased attention is a secondary gain for her, and in turn, a reason for her to resist recovery.

Most kids are unaware of the presence of secondary gains. However, these secondary gains are very powerful and can stop treatment progress and recovery from occurring. The therapist's ability to recognize resistance and the possibility of secondary gains is essential in helping the child to recognize her fears. Once the therapist can help the child connect her fears to her resistance, it is much easier to work with her effectively. For example, once this girl understood that she was resisting treatment out of fear that she might lose the attention she was finally receiving from her family, she was able to discuss her fears openly and receive reassurance that her parents' support would not end. The family worked hard to be more present for one another, and to support her through typical adolescent issues as well as when she was confronting a life-threatening illness.

Another common reason for relapse is *self-sabotage.* Self-sabotage is when the child puts herself in situation that will entice her to restrict, binge, purge or over-exercise. For example, if the person is seeking out the company of people whom she knows engage in eating-disordered behavior, she is placing herself at much greater risk of engaging in these behaviors too. Although she is often aware that she is placing extraordinary stress on herself, which she knows will be difficult, she does it anyway. Most often, individuals do this because they are not quite ready to give up their ED. In any case, it is a set-up for relapse and should be avoided until the person is far enough along in her recovery to withstand the influences of others. The therapist and the patient together can determine when this time would be.

Another possible reason for relapse is a *fear of change.* Change is hard for many people. The child may be losing part of her identity when she says good-bye to her ED. Remember individuals very much connect and identify with this illness. Because they see themselves as the illness, they have a hard time letting it go. Separation from it is part of the therapeutic work and often very difficult. For many people, their ED has been their best friend. When they are faced with losing it, they worry that they will be lost and alone. Many things in a person's life change when they rid themselves of their ED. Relationships may change, perspectives may change, and coping mechanisms may change. It is common to revert back to what is comfortable and familiar when faced with change, even if it is not healthy, because it *feels* safe.

Another reason for relapse is *distrust in recovery.* Even though caregivers know that the loss of ED behavior is for the better, the child may not fully believe this to be true. In the beginning of treatment, most individuals resist therapy because they believe that getting well means getting fat. Later in treatment, this distrust may or may not still be present. In either case, additional feelings of distrust may present themselves. The person is losing a coping mechanism that has served a purpose. Even with alternative coping mechanisms in place, she may not feel that these alternatives provide the same outlet for her needs. Patients need to be reminded that recovery is a process. It does not happen overnight. Therefore, if the child is used to a quick fix for her problems, when her needs are not met immediately she may revert back to old patterns because the new ones are "not working."

Lastly, having a low *deserve level* is another possible reason for relapse. The child may not believe that she deserves to get well. She may reject recovery due to continued low self-esteem and low self-confidence. Therefore, building up her deserve level is particularly important in treatment. The goal is to help the child increase her overall sense of self-worth.

RELAPSE PREVENTION

Anticipation and preparation are the best strategies in relapse prevention. Do not be afraid to talk to your child about her triggers. If you know what the triggers are, you can help your child anticipate the events, thoughts, and feelings that may lead to eating-disordered behaviors. Try to discuss ways that your child will be able to handle a potentially difficult scenario so that she does not fall into a state of crisis. You might role play or model ways in which she could cope with her distress. Coming up with alternative coping mechanisms ahead of time will help your child feel much more in control, and much less victimized, when dealing with potential struggles.

Initially, you may need to avoid triggers altogether. Although, this may not be ideal, it may be imperative in order for your child to resist relapse. For example, if you know that your child does not do well when she eats away from home, you may not be able to go out to a restaurant for a special birthday dinner. Instead, you may need to host the dinner at your home this year. Some parents get creative and have their child eat at home first, and then go to the restaurant with no worries if she cannot eat food there. However, this would not work if you wanted to go on a vacation where eating at home first would be impossible. It is highly probable that your child would not eat, lose weight, and potentially re-enter the hospital. I cannot tell you how many times I have worked with families who have attempted to go away for a week, but end up coming home early because their child has become medically unstable.

Changing plans and your lifestyle can be frustrating. If you are feeling annoyed, go back to what was discussed earlier in the book. Think about how you would react if your child had cancer. If she was in the midst of chemotherapy treatments that interfered with your family going to Hawaii for the week, would you be angry with her? You might be disappointed, but probably not as irritated and frustrated as in the case with her having an ED. Remind yourself that she did not ask for this illness and ultimately would prefer that things went back to the way they used to be. I doubt that she is happy with the fact that she will be missing out on a tropical vacation due to her eating disorder.

ENDING THERAPY

Termination of treatment should be well thought out and prepared for by the therapist. Typically, a therapist begins termination with a patient 4-6 weeks prior to their last appointment. This gives the therapist and patient enough time to discuss the work they accomplished, relapse prevention, and any other important details to support a successful end to therapy.

It is often very helpful for parents to ask their child's therapist what the termination policy is. This is important in case their child has a relapse or develops some other problem for which they need support. There is often a need to re-enter counseling for a check-in. Most therapists have what is called an *open-door policy*, which means that they are willing to see the patient again if a need arises. As a parent, you do not want to discourage further appointments if your child is struggling. Usually these types of appointments help to keep the person on track. They are not regular weekly sessions, but rather one or two appointments to guide and support the child intermittently.

It is not easy to overcome an eating disorder. Remember that you as parents are the best resource for your child. This is a difficult journey for the whole family. However, with your love, support, and guidance, your child has a much better chance of full recovery. In the next chapter, I would like to share with you some inspiring stories of treatment and recovery from the perspectives of different family members.

9

INSPIRING TRUE
STORIES OF RECOVERY

JESSICA, AGE 16

I was referred for counseling because within a six-month period, I lost 38 pounds. My doctor diagnosed me with Anorexia Nervosa, Binge-Eating/Purging Type. I am 5'9" tall with an ideal body weight of 145 pounds. The weight loss caused me to become "medically unstable," which I have come to understand means that your heart, temperature and blood pressure stink! I didn't think anything was wrong with me at first because I didn't really feel much different. I couldn't believe it when my doctor told me that my temperature was low and my heart rate was irregular. I thought my parents were crazy for making me go to the doctor in the first place. The doctor informed my parents that my heart rate was "alarmingly low," and that I was "at risk for cardiac arrhythmia and/or congestive heart failure." This seemed inconceivable to me since only a few hours before the appointment, I ran my best time ever at track practice, a time that would qualify me for Nationals.

I was even more shocked when my doctor told me she was sending me to the hospital. She said I had to go straight from her office. I wasn't even allowed to go home and get a toothbrush or clothes. I had never stayed overnight at a hospital before and I am not going to lie, it kind of freaked me out. I had no idea what to expect. The only time I had even ever been at a hospital was when I visited my dying grandfather. Certainly, I could not be in the same category as he was. Nothing was terribly wrong with me!

I tried to explain to my doctor and my parents that this was all a big mistake. I told them that I was training really hard for Nationals, and maybe I missed a meal or two here and there, but I could easily correct this if they did not make me go to the hospital. I pleaded with my dad who was an Olympic runner. I told him that if he followed the doctor's orders I would never make it to Nationals, which would ruin my chances for the Olympic tryouts. I told him it would be on his conscience that his daughter never got an Olympic medal and would live with that regret her whole life. I remember how he looked at me that night. He was torn between doing what he knew was best for me medically or giving me the chance to fulfill a lifelong dream. He had a personal understanding of the importance of seizing an opportunity to excel in sports when you can. There are many exceptionally talented athletes who never "make it" because of timing - their birth-date forces them to wait another year, or they miss a key event because of an unforeseen injury or personal circumstance.

In the end, my father decided to follow the doctor's recommendation, and he and my mother admitted me to the hospital. I had to stay there for two of the longest weeks of my life. In the hospital I quickly gained seven pounds, going from 107 to 114. I set it in my mind that I needed to gain weight as fast as I could to be released as soon as possible. All I could think about was exercising again and preparing for Nationals. It was not easy gaining the weight but I kept my eye on the ultimate goal; going to Nationals and maybe, just maybe, the chance to make the Olympic team.

As I gained the weight in the hospital, I realized how much I hated myself for getting sent to the hospital in the first place. I never wanted to be anorexic. It just happened. I will admit I wanted to be thin. I wanted to have virtually no body fat. I wanted to get rid of the extra weight that would slow me down. I liked seeing my lean body in the mirror. There were times I worried that my thighs were too large and my waist was too wide, but when I felt that way I fixed it by running extra miles that day. In the hospital I said and did all the right things so I could be released.

After I was discharged, I was forced by my parents to start individual therapy. My doctors instructed my parents to watch me every time I ate and make sure that I did not throw up my food. I couldn't believe the nerve of the doctors. I had never thrown up on purpose in my life. How dare they insinuate that I would start doing something like that? I was just a girl who had a dream, and that dream caused me to lose a little weight. What really made me furious is that the doctors also told my parents that I was not allowed to exercise until I gained five more pounds. They were worried that if I began to exercise, I would quickly lose the weight I gained in the hospital and have to be readmitted. This seemed unacceptable and outrageous to me. I also had to follow a strict meal plan set up by the nutritionist in the hospital, which put me at 2500 calories a day with NO EXERCISE. Were these people trying to make me fat? Was this some conspiracy to keep me from my dream?

I decided not to stand for it. I came up with a plan to keep the weight off without anyone knowing. I heard from another girl on the track team that there are websites that help girls with anorexia maintain their illness. They are called pro-ana websites. When I got home, I got on my computer and started surfing the web. I couldn't believe how many websites I found that promote eating disorders. I got some really good tips from them.

Before my first follow-up doctor's appointment, I drank a lot of water. I learned that the doctors would weigh me and that if I was water-logged, my recorded weight would be more than my actual weight. Unfortunately, my doctor eventually caught onto this and had me go to the bathroom before my weigh-in. So I went back to the websites and learned some new tricks. I began putting weights in my underwear. I taped them onto my skin. The doctor would weigh me in a gown but would allow my underwear to stay on. Unfortunately, one day they fell off my body when I was waiting for the nurse. She caught me and told my doctor despite all my pleading to keep my secret. Then I had to find a new hiding place for my weights. I had heard about girls putting them in their vaginas but I couldn't get up the nerve to try it. I was afraid that if I put the weights in, I might not be able to get them out. I was also worried that this would affect my running.

I started to worry that my waist was expanding so I read about a trick on a pro-ana website that said if I wrapped my waist and hips with Saran wrap before I went to bed, my body would mold to the wrap and stay lean and tight. I did this every night for several months before my mom caught me and started checking me in the middle of the night when I was sleeping. I am sorry to say that when many of the tricks I learned were discovered, I became more motivated to lose weight. I think I replaced my desire to be the perfect track star with the desire to be the perfect anorexic. My chances for Nationals and the possibility of the Olympics quickly faded and were replaced by my obsession with this illness.

I was determined to stay thin and avoid drawing attention to a problem that others insisted I had. At dinner time, I cut up food and moved it around on my plate to make it look like I was eating. When nobody was looking, I put pieces of food into my pockets to flush down the toilet after dinner. I often left crumbs on the floor for our dog to eat, knowing that these calories counted even if they were small amounts. I would even start fights with my family so that they would tell me to go to my room. The fights gave me the opportunity to storm out of the dining room while blaming them for causing me so much personal distress that I couldn't possibly eat another bite of food. I knew they felt guilty and blamed themselves for my problem. Although this made me feel bad for a moment, my own guilt quickly faded when I realized that it gotten me out of another meal. I began to see restriction of food as my greatest accomplishment.

Then one day the unexpected happened. I was exercising in my room (where it was less likely for my parents to catch me because I always had the music blaring to hide the noise of running in place, squats, push-ups and sit-ups) when I began having chest pains. At first I tried to justify the problem telling myself it was soreness from all the push-ups. However, the pain got worse. I started to get scared. I didn't know what to do. I was afraid to tell my parents because I knew they would be mad at me for sneaking in a workout. I tried lying down on my bed, but this made it worse. I felt dizzy and numb. I called out to my mom. She didn't hear me. I called out to my dad. He didn't hear me. My music was too loud and my voice was too soft. I could barely breathe. I reached for my cell phone but it fell on the floor. As I bent down to pick it up, I fell out of my bed and onto the floor. I was sweating and could feel myself growing weaker by the second. The pain was getting worse. I reached my cell phone and dialed 911. It was at that moment that I thought I was going to die.

The next thing I remember is waking up in a hospital room. I later found out that my sister heard a thud when I fell from my bed and knocked on my door. When I didn't answer, she went to get our parents. They broke the door down and found me passed out on the floor. The ambulance arrived and informed my parents that I had a heart attack. They rushed me to the hospital and were able to stabilize me. This was a huge wake-up call for me. It was probably the first time I actually admitted to myself that I had a problem.

When I was discharged from the hospital, I went to a residential treatment center for three months. In this program I worked on restoring my weight and addressing my body distortion issues. It was difficult to feel good about myself when all I could see in the mirror was a fat, ugly girl. I felt like an utter disappointment. There were several times that I thought about giving up and going back to my old tricks, but the look on my parents' faces and thought of how scared my little sister must have felt when she saw me lying on the floor kept me motivated. My sister is eight years old. She still has a hard time being around me because she is afraid of getting too close to someone that she could lose - at least that is what our family therapist explained. It is getting better though.

Following my stay at the residential treatment program, I came back home and began attending weekly individual, group, and family therapy in an outpatient setting. This is where I was really able to understand the reasons behind my eating disorder. I learned that I developed anorexia for a combination of reasons. I am a perfec-

tionist who will stop at nothing to achieve her goal. My
therapist helped me to use this quality to fight against my
illness instead of fighting for it.   The communication in
my family has greatly improved.   We were a very rigid
family with inflexible rules.   In family therapy, we all
learned how to be less rigid and more open and understanding of one another. I have a better relationship with
my parents now than ever before.   The relationship with
my little sister is still a work in progress. I am glad to be
alive. I know I was one of the lucky ones. I know my
recovery will be slow and gradual. I have learned to take
one day at a time. I have learned to ask my family for help
when I need it and to utilize my therapy sessions. I am
proud of how far I have come and excited to say that I am
in RECOVERY. Thank you for listening to my story.

JULIE, AGE 15

For as long as I can remember, I have been self-conscious about my weight. I think just about every teenage
girl is somewhat concerned about it; that's just normal.
But things can get really scary when something you think
is totally under your control turns into an obsession. It all
really started for me when I hit eighth grade, and I was
dying to lose weight. I was 5' 6" tall and weighed what I
thought was a disgusting 139 pounds. I had tried diets
and exercise in the past, but they would only last a few
weeks before I'd give them up. I had tried using my
mom's diet pills, but those weren't working either. I was
having a hard time at home with my family and at school
with friends and boyfriends, and suddenly I realized why

everything seemed to be going wrong for me; I was FAT! It was that simple.

I graduated from eighth grade that year trying to be happy, but feeling inside like I was huge. I spent all of my time comparing myself to my friends and other girls at my school who looked totally skinny. Why did my legs and butt have to be so big compared to theirs? Why couldn't I be a size 1 like they all were? I decided I had to do something about my weight. I went on a diet and lost a few pounds. I started counting calories like crazy. But that wasn't enough, and I wanted a faster way to lose weight. I started eating as little as possible. Every night I would think about what I had eaten that day, and feel totally guilty. If I had even eaten more than one bagel in a day, I would feel like I had failed. I tried chewing gum to feel like I was eating something, when I was really starving. Some days I would just eat nothing at all. If I did eat too much, I would run and run and run until I felt like maybe I had run off whatever I had just eaten. When I lost another five pounds, I felt like I was finally getting to the weight I wanted. But then over summer, I went to Hawaii, and by the time I got home I had gained three pounds. I felt like a disgusting failure.

I tried counting calories again, and running, but I always ended up eating more than I wanted to, and I wasn't losing that much weight. I was depressed and desperate. One day, I binged and ate so much that I felt sick. I panicked - I was totally pissed at myself and scared to death of gaining weight. I needed to get the food out of me and fast. I knew what Bulimia was and even though I had heard terrible stories about girls with eating disorders, I decided to see if it would work. No one was home so I went into the bathroom, stuck my finger down my throat, and finally made myself throw up. You would think I would feel gross and terrible, but I felt great. I walked out of the bathroom with a huge smile on my face that day, feeling like I had conquered the world. I knew right away that making myself throw up would not be just a one-time thing.

From then on, every time I felt like I had eaten too much I would purge, and every time I purged, I felt better and better. Whenever I craved the food I had been avoiding, I could eat whatever I wanted, and it wouldn't matter. It was like my guiltless way of eating and I loved it. Pretty soon, it was all I ever did and all I ever thought about. Every day when I went to school, I couldn't wait to get home so I could binge and purge again. I stopped having friends over to my house because they would only get in my way and I'd have to make up excuses about why I was spending so much time in the bathroom. I didn't care about anyone except myself and how much I weighed. I went from throwing up once a week to once every day and then up to four times a day.

I was overjoyed with how fast I lost weight. When I started purging I weighed 133 pounds. I went from 133 pounds to 129 and then from 129 pounds to 120. My size had gone from an 8 to a 2. I felt like I wasn't really putting myself in any real danger because none of my friends were saying anything. I figured my weight loss wasn't really noticeable. My family started to notice, however. My sister told me I had no butt at all and her friends constantly asked me how I was losing so much weight. They told me how skinny I was starting to look. It didn't make me feel bad to hear them say "Julie you are soooo skinny" because that's just what I wanted. It just made me more certain that I was accomplishing my goal. It didn't bother me to know that people thought I was too skinny. The weird thing was when I looked into the mirror, I did not see what they saw. I didn't see a skinny girl who needed to gain weight. I saw a fat girl who needed to lose a few more pounds. There was this little voice that came into my head constantly when I would eat or look in the mirror. It would say things like "Stop eating, you pig! You're eating so much more than anyone else! Guys don't like girls like that! You're going to get fat just like before!" But I honestly still believed I would know when I had lost enough weight and when I should stop purging. I thought I had total control.

Then one night, I don't even remember why, I cried out for help and I told my mother I was bulimic. She did some research and learned that Stanford had an eating disorder clinic. Since we lived nearby, she made an appointment for me to get an evaluation. However, the soonest they could get me in was in two or three months. I was glad it was going to be another couple of months before I got help because I would have more time to lose weight and binge and purge. I continued to throw up constantly, eating bigger and bigger amounts of food each time. I would make up excuses to bake brownies and then eat the whole batch myself. I would sneak ingredients into my room, make cookie dough on my bedroom floor, eat it all in one night and then throw it up in my bathroom when I was done. I would eat huge bowls of ice cream, slices or cake, pizza pies, and anything else I could get my hands on. I was completely out of control and felt totally helpless. It was like once I got into my room with food, I couldn't stop myself. I didn't even need to use my finger to throw up anymore. My body had gotten so used to throwing up that all I had to do was bend over and the food would come up automatically.

My parents were aware of the problem, but I got really good at hiding it. I continued to sneak food into my room to eat when they thought I was doing homework. I would run the water in the sink or shower to hide the sounds of vomiting after I ate. I began to clog toilets with all the throwing up I was doing so I had a plunger hidden under my bed and became my own plumber when I had to. Then I thought of a brilliant idea. I could eat as much food as I wanted, purge into a plastic bag, and let the bag float in the toilet until the next morning when I would dump it into a trash can at school. I hid the bags of vomit in my backpack until I could get to the nearest garbage. On hot days, it would smell more so I often ran the bags over to a neighbor's trash can. As disgusting as this may sound, it seemed like the most brilliant idea ever because it allowed me to continue purging without detection.

My sister was aware of the problem as well. She often complained to our parents that there was no food in the house. I couldn't blame all the missing food on my friends, because I wasn't inviting them over any more. I couldn't blame it on her friends (although once I tried) because she was with them when they were at our house and saw exactly what they were eating. I started eating food that nobody would suspect me of eating. Things only my dad would eat so nobody would notice it was missing and blame me. I also started going to grocery stores and opening bags and boxes of food in the aisle to eat as I strolled through the store. I never bought anything because I had no money and no need.

Pretty soon I began to see all the scary effects of constant binging and purging and weight loss. For one thing, I hadn't gotten my period for five months. My skin was so dry, it actually hurt. All the color had left my face, and my eyes looked sunken. I was constantly tired and had no energy at all. When I ran in my PE class, I would feel like I was going to pass out. My throat hurt constantly and I was always freezing cold. I started growing extra hair on my arms because my body couldn't keep itself warm. I remember being so happy because my hip bones were starting to stick out and I could see my rib cage through my skin. I lost another 10 pounds, getting down to 110 and a size 0. I still thought I was fat though. When I looked in the mirror, I still didn't see the skinny, sunken-in girl that I really was, I still saw the fat girl.

At a family Christmas party, all my relatives noticed my drastic weight loss, and started talking about it. I was incredibly angry that they said I looked BAD. I had worked so hard and put my life at risk to be skinny, how could they say I didn't look good? I figured they were just jealous. When I went out to dinner one night, the waiter asked my friend, who was working as a waitress, if I had an eating disorder because I looked so frail. When I heard this I completely lost it. I was so confused. How could random people who had never even seen me before know that I was anorexic and bulimic? This is when I realized that I really had a problem. I didn't want to look as bad as people were saying I looked. Instead of being afraid of gaining weight, sometimes I felt afraid of losing weight because I didn't want people to say that I looked terrible. I was totally stuck. Inside, I was afraid of being fat, but everyone around me was afraid because I was so skinny. I was so confused and I didn't know what to do.

One morning while taking a shower, my hair started falling out. I cried the whole day. This is when I finally realized that I needed to get better. I was sick of everyone saying "Julie, you look sooooo skinny" because now I knew everyone really thought I looked bad. I was tired of having to buy new clothes every weekend because none of my clothes ever fit me anymore. They were always too big or too small. I was scared to death of losing my hair. I was tired of my sister being angry with me when I did throw up and I was sick of all my friends not understanding!! I was sick of going to Stanford (I finally got into the clinic) and counseling every week. I just wanted to be normal and to have my life back.

But when I tried to stop purging, I couldn't. I was addicted. I was never happy if I couldn't throw up. I lashed out at my family when they would try to talk to me about it. I felt like being able to throw up was all I had left. I tried so hard just to go one day without purging, but

I couldn't. I would restrict food the whole day, and then at night I would always binge, which would lead me to throwing up again. It sounds so simple to just not throw up, because I knew it was killing me, but when I was in the moment, I would tell myself it was okay and that I would do it this one last time and then I would get better. It was a vicious cycle that I just couldn't break.

After weeks of this, I talked to my mom about it because I felt so bad about myself. I felt helpless, ugly, and suicidal. I wanted to go to a residential treatment program where I would have no choice but to get better. That's when my mom called Dr. Krautter. We started seeing her as a family, so that I wouldn't have to go to a residential treatment program. Instead, my family started working in outpatient family therapy together. They began monitoring what I ate and made sure I did not purge. Dr. Krautter used a family therapy approach called the Maudsley model. It is where parents "re-feed their child." Sounds crazy right? At first I didn't like the sound of it, but it was a way for my family to create a type of residential program in my own home.

Even though I hated it at the time, because I wanted to binge and purge so badly, in the long run, it gave me the structure I needed to get better. The pantry where we kept our food in our house was locked up, so that even when I was craving food, I couldn't binge. That was probably the hardest time for me, but I started getting a whole lot better. I got my purging down to only once a week. Because my metabolism was so messed up by that time, I easily got back up to 115 pounds. My skin was a lot less dry, the color was coming back into my face, my eyes didn't look so sunken in, and I had a little bit more energy. I even started losing less hair. But for weeks, I stayed stuck at purging once a week. I knew the eating disorder had much less control over me, but in a way, I didn't want to totally let it go. It was as if it was my best friend. So I kept throwing up just that one time a week. As long as I still purged, I knew that I had my friend, and would not gain too much weight.

Finally, I was able to really make a firm decision that I just couldn't do this anymore and I pushed myself to stop purging altogether. With my family and friends' help, with support from Dr. Krautter, and with my own determination, I finally broke the habit. Once I hit 118 pounds, I got my period back. This was scary, but also encouraging because it meant that I was finally getting my life back. I am so proud to say that I haven't thrown up for over six months now. Everyday I am getting stronger and I think less and less about purging. I truly do not believe that I will ever purge again. I now weigh 122 pounds and am a size 4. I am getting pretty comfortable with myself and my body image. My skin is healthy again and my hair has finally stopped falling out. I have been getting my period regularly for several months now. I can exercise regularly too now that I have more energy, and it does not feel like a chore anymore.

I know that I am not totally better yet. I still have bad days. Sometimes when I look in the mirror a little part of me still sees that fat girl I still get upset when I eat too much, but I am not counting calories or restricting food anymore. Instead, I am trying to listen to my stomach and what my body needs and does not need. However, it is not uncommon for me to hear that little voice in my head that says I am fat. With the help of my therapist, I have learned how to shut that voice out. I have realized that very few teenage girls are a size 1. I have learned that I don't have to be 100 pounds to be beautiful. I hang out with my friends again, now that binging and purging isn't all that I want to do. I have a life again, and my weight isn't constantly on my mind. Six months ago my eating disorder took over my life, but I am very proud to say that I have taken it back. I realize how lucky I am. I never was hospitalized and never ended up going to a residential treatment center. More importantly, I came out of this alive and I am so thankful for that because I know how many girls aren't that lucky.

WILLIAM, AGE 17

I started struggling with Anorexia when I was 14 years old. I am the youngest in a large family. I have three older brothers and two older sisters. My family is very religious and close-knit. Although many of my siblings have families of their own, they all live close by, and spend lots of time at my parents' house visiting. It is important to my parents that we all stay connected. My family is also very focused on success. My parents have a strong work ethic, which they passed down to all their kids including me. Among my siblings there a few doctors, a lawyer, a professor, and a research assistant at Harvard (where she attends currently). I am a senior in high school. I have a

4.5 GPA and I struggle for perfection in my grades, body image, and basketball skills Due to problems with malnutrition and weight loss, I was not able to pursue basketball. However, I was able to focus on my grades and my weight.

Most people think it is weird for a guy to have an eating disorder. In fact, that is probably why it took my family so long to become aware of the problem. I also worked really hard at hiding it. I think this is because I was embarrassed and ashamed. I have never known any of my guy friends to worry about their weight or get upset because they thought their thighs and stomachs looked fat. It felt really "girly" and not something you would hear from a jock. So I kept it a secret from everyone.

When I started losing weight, I hid it by wearing extra clothes and baggy pants. This worked until I had my annual physical. My pediatrician said that I had lost 40 pounds since last year. With a growth spurt, my parents noticed that I "thinned out." However, they thought that was normal. A lot of kids thin out when they are growing and maturing. My doctor asked me if I was eating differently and I told him "no, just exercising more." He agreed with my parents that it was probably a growth spurt, and since I was medically stable, he told them not to worry.
He did note that since I was on the thin side, I should probably increase my caloric intake. He made a joke about how lucky I was to be a growing boy with a fast metabolism who could eat whatever he wanted and not gain a pound.

I was ecstatic that I fooled all of them including my doctor. I had no intention to eat more and gain weight. In fact, the thought of it caused such anxiety that I pushed it out of my mind completely. Instead, I focused on ways to maintain my restricting behavior. It actually wasn't that hard for me to do. The thought of food and eating repulsed me most of the time, which made me lose my appetite. In addition, if I experienced hunger pains, I convinced myself that they represented the loss of unnecessary fat on my legs and stomach. Without food, this fat would disappear and never come back. That thought helped me not to eat. Restricting food demonstrated the strength of my will power and motivation to achieve my goal.

I continued to hide the problem from my family and friends, but eventually they found out that I was not simply in the midst of a growth spurt. The fact that I kept losing weight and not getting any taller was a sure giveaway. Then something rather dramatic occurred that really confirmed my parents' suspicions. I was 15 years old and playing in an out-of-state basketball tournament. My parents and some of my siblings flew out to watch the championship game. Right in the middle of the game, I fainted. Just went down, right on the court. Afterwards, I tried to convince my parents that I was simply tired from staying up late the night before, studying for a test I had on Monday. But they didn't buy it. Paramedics came to the gym, checked my vital signs, and took me to the hospital where I was admitted for medical instability. My heart rate was low, my temperature was low and I was dehydrated.

At the hospital, it became apparent to my family how little food I was actually consuming. They saw the fear in my eyes when the nurses brought me meals. They saw the distress in my body after I ingested high caloric foods. I decided to tell them the truth. I reluctantly explained to all of them that I had been struggling with an eating disorder for over a year, and doing my best to hide it from them as well as from my coach, my teachers, and my friends. My parents were shocked, angry and confused. However, they did what my parents have always done for all their kids when a problem arose; they moved into "fix it" mode.   From the hospital, they made telephone calls and found a counselor for me to work with individually as well as a family counselor. When I was released from the hospital, I flew home and immediately started going to both individual and family therapy sessions on a weekly basis. I also had weekly doctor and nutritionist appointments.

I was in therapy for two years before I reached full recovery. I am now 17 years old. Recovery was a slow process for me. I can't tell you how hard it is to overcome the power of an eating disorder. I also can't pretend I know exactly what to tell you to do to help your own kids because everyone is different. But I can tell you what worked and didn't work for me. Hopefully, sharing my story with you will give you some guidance.

First, let me start with what didn't work. When I was criticized and expected to get better overnight it definitely did not help. As I mentioned earlier, my family is very hard working and they move into action mode when there is a problem. They were hoping for - expecting really - a quick resolution. When this didn't happen, they got frustrated. And that frustration was directed at me. They were angry and scared and said things like, "Get over it! Just eat something." And even though they meant well, it made me feel worse when they would say, "You are killing yourself and ruining our family." Trust me when I say that if it was that easy to eat food and get over my eating disorder, I would have. I didn't want to be the cause of all this stress in my family.

Most people don't understand how difficult it really is to overcome an eating disorder because they are not the one going through it. Often times, you know that without food, you could die, but you cannot find a way to help yourself and eat. It is as if something is forcing you to deny yourself food. I often felt totally out of control and helpless to stop the restricting and over-exercising.

For a long time, I tried to fight my eating disorder all by myself because I didn't feel like people understood me. I isolated myself, which made things worse because when I was alone, the urge to restrict and over-exercise was stronger. There were times when I believed people in my life didn't care. Even though I was good at hiding my problem, I thought if people really cared about me they would notice and try to get me some help. In looking back, I think a lot of people probably did notice but had no idea what to say. Or maybe they were just afraid to say the wrong thing.

You definitely want to be careful what you say to a person with an eating disorder. A lot of times people say the wrong things even when they are trying to be helpful. For example, my parents thought they were being encouraging when they would say things like "Good job! You ate so much tonight." These types of comments almost always make the person with an eating disorder think, "You ate so much, you fat slob, even your parents noticed." When my parents told me how well they thought I was doing in my treatment, I interpreted it to mean that I was getting fat. This completely freaked me out and made me obsess about what I had eaten. I would think about all the calories I consumed that day or week and then beat myself up mentally for eating way too much food and causing weight gain. Parents are better off saying neutral things to their kids when they are in treatment and recovery.

There are many things that my parents did that were helpful. What I needed most was support. I needed my family and friends to understand me and encourage me in a way that was not blameful and/or critical. I needed them to tell me that I was doing a great job, not because of the food that I was eating, but because of the courage it took to move forward and make changes in my life. Any type of focus on food felt scary and bad to me. It helped when my parents told me they were proud of me. It helped when my siblings told me that they were impressed with my motivation for change. When I did start to gain weight, I really liked that they did not comment on how healthy I looked now. These comments would have put the focus back on food, weight and body image and would have freaked me out.

I remember one time when my sister was home from college and she came into my room and told me that she was so glad that I was her brother. She told me how amazing I was and how I inspired her to work on herself. You have no idea how much that encouraged me to stay on top of my eating disorder and fight the urges to relapse. Sometimes it really is the little things people say that make a difference.

Another thing that really helped me was structure. I needed structure in my life around food, and as hard as it was for me and as much as I didn't like having so much attention on my eating, I don't think I could have recovered without it. I needed someone to take control of the situation, and of me, when I couldn't do it for myself. My parents monitored everything I ate, and watched over me all the time. I am not going to lie, I was incredibly angry about this and they knew it. I cussed at them, slammed doors and threatened to run away. One night I even threatened to hurt myself if they didn't stop treating me like a prisoner. However, my parents just did what they were instructed to do. They told me they loved me, stayed with me when I threatened to hurt myself, and monitored my food intake and exercise. In the end, it worked. I realized that they were doing this because they were not going to let me die. They saved my life.

Another thing that really helped was family therapy. During the sessions, we all began to communicate better and understand why this illness infiltrated our lives in the first place. The therapist taught us how to work together as a family to fight against the eating disorder. I always thought I would have to fight it on my own. I was wrong. My family learned how to be an incredible resource for me. They stopped fighting me and started fighting with me against the illness.

In particular, the therapist taught my parents to direct their anger toward the illness. She told them that they had every right to be angry. She reminded them that this was an aggressive illness that could have deadly consequences. She said most parents are furious that their child has developed this illness, and that the family as a whole is affected by it. But then she talked to them about externalizing the problem so that the anger was placed on the right target - the illness; not on me, the family member suffering from the illness.

She also talked to me about how I was also targeting the wrong thing too. My parents weren't the only ones blaming me for having an eating disorder. I blamed myself for causing everyone in my family so much pain.   I also totally identified myself with the illness. By doing so, I took it on as my identity. Anorexia was not a problem I had, but who I was. This made it much harder to fight against. Through therapy, I began to separate myself from the illness. The intervention helped me to realize that the eating disorder is not who I am as a person, but simply a problem that I am facing and one that I now had motivation to get rid of it.

One last thing that I think was very helpful was the realization that an eating disorder is just like any other disease. Dr. Krautter once asked my parents in a session when they were being accusatory and critical, whether they would act this way towards me if I had cancer. My whole family got really silent and my mom started to cry. I think that was the first time that they really understood that I did not ask for this illness, I did not want this illness, and I needed to fight for my life against this illness. I thought about it that night in bed. I asked myself "Would you ever get pissed off with someone for having cancer and expect them to just get over the illness or deal with it on their own because it was destroying the family?" The answer was a big fat NO.

One of the hardest things for me to do was to fight against anorexic thinking - the little voices that would tell me I was fat. Many people think that eating disorders end once you gain the weight back. They definitely don't. To battle this, whenever I felt like I was fat, I would grab my basketball and go shoot hoops. I was tall enough to dunk and often practiced dunking. I would pretend that every time I crushed ball through the hoop, I slammed the illness down. As stupid as it may sound, honestly, it helped.

I had a lot of trouble understanding what a "normal, healthy meal" looked like. It was helpful for my family to illustrate this for me because I constantly worried I was eating too little or too much. At dinner I would ask my parents if what was on my plate looked pretty average to them, and they would tell me honestly if I needed to eat just a little more or just a little less. This was important in the beginning when I was getting back to normal eating. Later, I was able to listen to my body and decide what I needed.   Knowing that I wasn't totally over under-eating or over-eating lowered my anxiety at mealtimes, and helped me not feel like I need to restrict or over-exercise afterwards.   Having a nutritionist monitor my eating habits and put me on a meal plan also helped a lot.

Weigh-in can be tricky at the doctor's office.   Some people don't like to know what their weight is because if they gain they will freak out.   Seeing a number on a scale that is not what you are expecting can be terrifying.   I wanted to know my weight.   It helped me to know that the amount of food I was consuming was not causing me to gain 100 pounds.   I remember the first time I asked to see my weight was after a lunch where, despite my better judgment, I had some chocolate for desert.   I was sure that the chocolate caused me to gain ten pounds.   When I stepped on the scale and saw that I did not gain an ounce, I realized that I actually might be able to eat and enjoy some foods that, in the past, were frightening for me.

Finally, I was motivated by the consequences of eating disorders and seeing some of the effects on my own body. I had no idea that what I was doing was so dangerous.   I didn't think it was that big of a deal.   But once my body began to break down, I began to want to get better.   Probably the biggest motivation was when I lost the energy to play basketball.   I wanted to get better, not become weak and listless.   Being malnourished and dehydrated caused me to play terribly.   And then, as I described above, I reached the point where I couldn't play at all.   Who wants a kid in the championships who might faint in the middle of a game?   Nobody.   Certainly not college scouts.

I hope my story helps you to better understand the hard work that goes into recovering from an eating disorder. I always thought it was a problem that only girls faced. And I thought it was an individual struggle. However, after what I went through, I have a better understanding of how this illness affects boys and the family as a whole. What we went through as a family made us all stronger and closer to one another. I didn't think that could happen, considering we were a pretty close family to begin with, but it did. There was more support and understanding, and most of all, more patience and acceptance. I wouldn't wish this illness on anyone but I am glad to have my family so close. I know they love me and will support me through the toughest of times. If your child is struggling, never give up. He or she needs you.

KARLY, AGE 16

Hi my name is Karly. I am 16 and a junior in high school. I have been struggling with Anorexia Nervosa for about three years now. From what I can remember, my eating disorder first started up when I was at the end of 8th grade. At the time, I weighed 160 pounds and was very self-conscious about my body. I was taller than most, but 160 pounds was still a lot for my height. My parents were constantly telling me that I needed to lose weight, and people would judge me based on my looks, and make fun of me behind my back. All I wanted was to be part of the popular crowd and I wanted to be envied by the girls whom I had envied for long. I wanted a boyfriend, but I felt like no guy was ever going to want to be with me when I was fat, ugly, and unattractive.

Around April of 8th grade, I started dieting and eating really healthy. I was playing volleyball at the time, and through diet and exercise, I started to lose weight. By the end of the season, I had lost about 30 pounds. People were complimenting me on how I looked and it felt amazing to be noticed finally. As soon as volleyball season was over, I stopped losing weight and even started to put some back on. People stopped complimenting me on how good I looked, and I missed the sense of self-worth that their compliments gave me. I decided that I was willing to do absolutely anything to get skinny and to stay skinny, even if it meant hurting myself in the process.

It is weird; I knew that what I might do to myself would jeopardize my health, which a lot of people say they were unaware of when they look back on their illness. I was very aware, but didn't care. That is when my eating disorder made its first appearance. By summer, I was going up to a day without eating anything and I was weighing myself every time I used the bathroom and then some. Sometimes, I would try throwing up but it never worked, so I decided to just keep on not eating. My weight loss was evident and I was getting noticed again, but in my mind I could never be noticed enough.

My freshman year at high school started and things started to get back in order for me. I was playing volleyball and could eat normally and still lose weight because of the amount of calories I was burning while playing. Once that stopped, I started gaining weight again and stopped eating to lose the weight that I had gained. I also started throwing up every time I ate something, because at times I had no choice but to eat. I learned how to throw up from a website. It is amazing how much information you can get on the web for things that can be really bad for you. Apparently, nobody monitors this.

I know my parents had no idea what I was doing. I hated the way I looked and I would say nasty things to myself in the mirror as motivation to keep myself from eating. I would call myself ugly and fat and constantly put myself down and say that I wasn't good enough and that I was never going to be liked unless I lost weight. After telling myself that I was worthless over and over again, it became fixed in my head and I actually believed it. My best friend eventually told my parent what was going on with me, even after I promised her that I would stop, but by then it was too late. I was hooked on the eating disorder and attention it gave me, and I was not in any position to give it up. My parents would try to make me eat, but I would either refuse to eat it or eat it and then go purge. Every singe thing I ate either ended up in my pockets, my sleeves, or down the drain.

I was going to the doctor weekly to monitor my weight and heart rate, and at 123 pounds, my heart became too weak and I was sent to the hospital. At night, my heart rate would go so low that I could have died at any second, but to be honest, I really didn't care. I stayed there for eight days while the doctors monitored my heart and had me gain weight.

Two days after getting out of the hospital, I was back to not eating and throwing up everything that I did eat. The rest of my freshman year was a downward spiral. I continued to lose weight while slipping into a deep depression. I would isolate myself from others and allow my eating disorder to take over. When I couldn't get away with restricting food or throwing up because my parents were suspicious, I did something I thought I would never do in a million years. I cut myself. It made me feel better. It numbed the stress I was feeling when I couldn't have my eating disorder.

The anxiety in my life was high. I felt like everyone was judging me and nobody understood me. If I ate something because my parents forced me to, then I would hurt myself as a punishment. I was losing my friends, my family and most of all, myself. Sometimes I would ask myself "What are you doing?" The answer was almost always the same, I was doing what I had to do to look good and to survive. Later I would ask myself at what price? My weight had gotten down to 108 pounds and my mind and body were starting to suffer. My hair was falling out, I had lost my period, I was always cold, I had no energy and was always tired. I was alone and depressed, and I just wanted to starve myself to death and end all the suffering I had caused myself and others.

During the summer before my sophomore year of high school, I decided that I had had enough. I was sick and tired of my day revolving around food and weight, and the constant thoughts were ruining my summer and destroying any chance of having a good school year to come. On night, I sat my parents down in tears and asked them to send me to a treatment center to get help because I just couldn't do it by myself. I wanted my life back and I wanted to live the way a teenager should. I went to residential program in Utah for two-and-a-half months, where I learned to become accepting of my disease and of my body. I was able to nourish myself back to health and rebuild some of the relationships that I had ruined during my eating disorder.

I thought that I was ready to leave treatment early, so I talked my parents into it, and they took me out against the recommendation of my doctors. After returning home from Utah, I was back to hardly eating anything within the first week. When I got home I weighed 130 pounds and within 3 months I weighed 110 and was back in the hospital. I was extremely depressed again and was back to isolating myself and cutting. When I got out of the hospital, at first I only came out of my room to go to school and to use the bathroom. I avoided my family and friends at all costs.

However, despite all of this, I was able to gain some weight back. This helped me to make some better decisions. It is weird how when you are completely malnourished, you make really bad decisions. It is as if you are in a cloud and cannot think clearly. I wanted to be in recovery, but I continued to struggle with how to make this happen.

My parents found me a really good therapist whom I started to see on a weekly basis. During my treatment with her, I started understanding the illness. I learned to utilize as many support systems as possible. I started really eating healthy again and exercising when feeling bloated or overwhelmed. My doctors allowed me to exercise because I had gained enough weight for it to be healthy and safe. I am not going to lie, recovery has been a roller coaster for me. Currently, I am working on accepting who I am no matter what my weight is. I know deep inside that my life can't be run by a number on a scale. I am who I am and if people, guys in particular, can't accept that, then maybe I don't want those kinds of people in my life.

Each and every day is a struggle for me and every morning I have to ask myself "Do I want this today?" Some days, than answer is "No", but those days are rare and my will to get my life back overpowers the weakness. I still have to constantly battle the thoughts in my head to restrict my food and to lose weight, but I have learned to stand up against the thoughts and talk back to them. I know that I never want my life to go back to the way it was for the past three years. I want to live like a normal teenager, and if eating disordered thought are constantly in my head I am never going to live my life in peace.

I look back on my life with this disease and it makes me sad to think that I've basically thrown away some of the best years of my childhood. Obsessing over weight and food and calories is not a way to live your life and I only wish I had known this back then before it was too late. I'd give anything to do it all over again and do it right, but I can't turn back time and I am just thankful to be alive and to still have the love and support of my friends and family.

I want to encourage anyone out there to get help before you lose yourself in this disease. I know the people reading this book are parents. My biggest advice to you is that if you have a child that is struggling with an eating disorder, you should get them in to see someone who can help them right away. My parents didn't realize how bad things were for me because I hid it so well. Most kids with an eating disorder work really hard to keep the problem a secret. My parents minimized the problem because I convinced them that it wasn't a big deal even though it was. They had no idea how hard I was struggling. It is very hard to fight this illness on your own, and even though your kid will tell you they can, they probably can't. I don't know anyone who has been able to do it on their own. Once kids realize that they don't have to do it on their own, they will be relieved. They will be mad at first that you are trying to help them, but trust me; they will thank you in the long run.

My therapist has asked me to share my story with others. When I speak to other teenagers I often end my talk by saying that there is nothing glamorous about anorexia or bulimia and that being skinny has nothing to do with being happy. It is the people around you that make you happy. We all have the rest of our lives ahead of us, and we need to all realize that we are beautiful just the way we are.

ALICIA'S MOTHER

I am not sure where to begin in writing about the point of view or experience of a parent of a daughter with anorexia. I can remember back to before it all started and remember how she was – always happy and full of laughter, busy with school and cheerleading, and always out with lots of friends. She was a good student, an incredible athlete, and very popular at school. She was a good dancer too. I remember her always doing spins or choreographing dance moves in the kitchen. She would also do back handsprings or back walkovers down the hallway. She was always in motion. She was the most graceful and powerful person I knew. I miss seeing her like that. Even as a baby and young girl, she had always been happy and full of life and energy.

Three-and-a-half years ago, it all started to unravel. She was a freshman in high school and started losing weight. I naïvely thought it was the typical dieting that all high school girls do. She was always out with friends and would say she had eaten a lot with them and so wasn't very hungry for dinner. Then she began cutting her food into microscopic pieces. My husband started to express some concerns, but I was still sure it was nothing. To this day, I cannot forgive myself for not seeing all the signs. It wasn't until a family vacation at Easter time, when we were with her for all meals and saw her in a bathing suit, that we knew there was something terribly wrong.

When we returned home, I contacted my daughter's pediatrician and was told to bring her in for a check-up. She warned me that they might have to put my daughter in the hospital. I just couldn't believe that my daughter could be that sick. How naïve and stupid I was. At the office, the doctor came out and told us that Alicia was in bradycardia at 35 beats per minute. She was going to call Stanford's Eating Disorder unit and try to get her in. She met the criteria: low body weight (she weighed 86 lbs.), low body temperature, low heart rate. My husband and I were in shock. When we went in to tell Alicia that she was going to the hospital, she was shocked too, but too weak to fight it.

We arrived at the hospital and checked her in. I did not know anything about eating disorders and couldn't believe that there were so many girls and boys struggling with this illness. I was even more amazed to find out that there was a whole hospital ward set up for them. My husband and I were now entering a world we were not prepared for and were completely ignorant about. Upon admission, Alicia was put on strict bed rest, connected to a heart monitor, and started on a liquid diet. They called it "re-feeding".

I didn't understand why they didn't give her regular food until I saw the distress she experienced just drinking 2. 8 oz. of a nutritional drink called Boost. She was totally stressed out with the demands of consumption and became very nasty to everyone around her. I had never seen my daughter say a mean thing to anyone in her life. She was always very respectful of everyone. That all changed in the hospital. She was belligerent and cussed out doctors, nurses and dieticians. She looked like my daughter, but acted like someone I didn't know. It was like she was possessed, especially when food was mentioned.

My husband and I were beside ourselves to see this change. We met with the doctor and were told that Alicia had Anorexia Nervosa. We thought, "great, now give her

the medicine or operation and let's get this over with."
We were so ignorant to think it would be so simple to
cure. We started a crash course in eating disorders through books, lectures, and meetings with doctors
and nurses. But we still didn't really understand the road
we were about to travel. Alicia was in the hospital for four
weeks on a liquid diet. She became extremely anxious and
began having severe anxiety attacks. The psychiatrist put
her on medication but it didn't seem to help. She would
get into the fetal position and moan and then begin to
hyperventilate. It scared us to death. No one seemed to be
able to help when these attacks occurred.

One day at the hospital, Alicia was on the floor having a
bad panic attack and we were talking to her and trying to
get her to focus on us, but we couldn't reach her. Thank
God that the canine visitors came. They provide dog
therapy to patients who are struggling with severe emotional distress. A big Great Dane came in and sat down
right next to her. He nuzzled Alicia's hand and she began
to pet him. This simple connection brought her back to
us. To this day, when I think of our desperation in trying
to reach Alicia in her pain, the picture in my mind of that
dog sitting next to her and her looking up at him still
brings tears to my eyes. That dog did what we could not
do.

Unfortunately, the dog could not stay with her forever,
and the panic attacks continued as Alicia was given more
to drink or eat in her hospital bed. She refused to drink
water and every time the dietician tried to increase her
food intake, the nastiness that my daughter displayed

became worse, as well as her choice of words. She even threatened the night nurse with wrapping the feeding tube around his neck and strangling him. Where did our daughter go and who was this possessed girl?? We thought that the staff must think we were terrible parents to raise such a nasty daughter. How could we begin to explain what our daughter was really like and how much we missed her?

After four weeks, Alicia was released. We were to do the "Maudsley" method of family therapy. Due to her history of both restricting food as well as purging what little she did eat, we were instructed by the hospital staff to have every meal with her and then sit with her for two hours after each meal and snack. We needed to find a therapist for her and keep her weekly medical appointments at the Eating Disorder Outpatient Clinic. Alicia lasted three days at home before she was readmitted to the hospital.

The first words from the doctor were, "I thought she would have made it at least a week before coming back." We realized that they knew she was not ready to leave the hospital, but their hands were tied with the insurance companies. If the patient is medically stable, even if the doctor knows the patient is not ready to leave, they have to discharge them, even knowing that they will be back in a matter of days. This was the beginning of our enlightenment about the American medical system. We would learn a lot more about it as we navigated the gray area of mental disorders.

Alicia spent another week in the hospital. The panic attacks continued and she wrote in her journal that she

wanted to kill herself. She was now on suicide watch. The
doctors said that Alicia's Anorexia was severe and she was
not ready to leave the hospital, but they would have to
release her because she was technically medically stable.
They knew that she would be back in a matter of days
once again. They begged us to get her into a residential
program when she left the hospital as they knew she was
not going to make it at home. They called the only adolescent residential program in Northern California (six beds)
but the waiting time was two to three months. The only
available programs were in Southern California, Utah and
Arizona.

Alicia pleaded for us to take her home, and my husband, against the advice of the doctors and staff, promised
her that he would. She was released, even though she was
not even on solid food yet. We were given information
and a meal plan from the dietician. The doctors advised
us to remove all knives and medications from the home,
so she could not harm herself in any way. Alicia was sent
home and we had to be the ones to get her through this. I
had all but quit teaching, and my boss and colleagues were
wonderful in supporting me and giving me all the time off
that I needed. We were overwhelmed to say the least.
How were we going to ever get through this? There is so
little support and we were the ones that were supposed to
be her caregivers and help her heal. We were completely
out of our minds with worry and feelings of helplessness
and fear that we were too incompetent to help her, and
yet, her life depended on it.

Once home, it was evident we were fighting a losing battle. Our daughter stood at the table instead of sitting, and hyperventilated while she tried to eat. We were already falling behind in what she was supposed to eat on her meal plan. We had to be with her constantly, which was incredibly time consuming. She was so scared of eating that one meal or snack took her a long time to finish. In addition, we had to sit with her for two hours after eating, which meant that we had only one hour before we had to start the process all over again. This stressed the whole family. Alicia was so stressed that the anxiety attacks continued. We were in panic ourselves whenever one occurred because we felt helpless to stop them. I remember wondering if our lives would ever be the same again. I wished we could go back in time, and I promised myself to never undervalue the beauty of a simple, uneventful day.

By day two, it was obvious that Alicia would be back in the hospital as she could not eat enough to sustain herself. I decided to call and see if there was any way to get her into a residential program in LA. They had an opening in Lakewood and we needed to get her there the following day. We made the decision to not let her know our plans to take her due to her high stress levels. She had not done well when this possibility was discussed in the hospital, and there she had a support team to help her and monitor her. We were worried that this information would send her over the edge or cause her to run away.

It was the worst thing we have ever done, and to this day I hate myself for it and I hate this disease for making me even have to consider such a thing. I have always been honest with my children. It was the most dishonest thing I have ever done, but I felt that we had no other options. We weren't doctors or therapists but simply parents. We had no idea what we were doing and what this illness was about.

We woke Alicia up after midnight and told her we were taking her to the residential treatment center in LA. She began crying and pleading. It hurt us to see her so devastated, and it broke our hearts to hear her pleas. What kind of parents do this to their daughter? I suppose, very desperate parents who listen to what the doctors tell them to do.

We arrived in Lakewood by 8 am and entered the residential treatment center. We were met by the staff who immediately went through Alicia's bags and got her settled in her room. The first time that we had to leave her in Lakewood, I felt sad, guilty and like a failure as a parent. I knew she probably hated us for doing what we did and I understood her feelings. The schedule while she was there was that we were allowed to visit her on Sundays, from 1 to 5 pm, and then we would spend the night to be at family therapy on Monday mornings. We drove down every weekend for five weeks. During the week we read more books and tried to learn as much as we could about eating disorders. We did not know anyone else who had gone through this disease. We felt alone and emotionally wrecked.

Family therapy provided by the residential treatment center was painful. We felt guilty and overwhelmed with grief and Alicia was angry with us. Everyone's emotions were raw. Her brother came too and he was the only one she trusted. When we talked to her on the phone, I could hear the anger in her voice. At one point she threatened to quit eating if we didn't get her out of there. I struggled with this and nearly gave in except that I realized she was trying to blackmail us so I told her that if she quit eating then she would be placed in a hospital down there, not up in the Bay Area. I think at that point she decided to play the game to get out of there. Her plan was to gain the weight and then get out and come home, dump the weight and leave home. She now saw us as the enemy.

Alicia came home in August. The residential therapists recommended that she attend an intensive outpatient program in San Francisco, 3 to 4 times per week. We commuted back and forth to San Francisco for four months. She hated every therapist and dietician that worked there. She re-assumed her rude and unpleasant behavior. For us as parents, the outpatient program was extremely helpful. We did not have any local support. We wanted to understand what anorexia really was and we needed someone to answer our questions. This place at least gave us a family support group, family therapy, and information about anorexia. It helped us to talk with other parents who were also on this path. We were just beginning to understand what we were dealing with.

The family support group kept me sane. I could say the things I felt and there were other parents that could relate. We were just beginning to realize how long the road to recovery could take and we were trying desperately to find our daughter, the sweet, affectionate, happy girl we had always known. She was still nowhere to be seen. Alicia was still losing weight, lying to us, and planning to emancipate herself. She did find and choose a therapist that she researched while in Lakewood, and also began seeing her. We also began a new approach, the "modified Maudsley" which consisted of being with her at two meals to let her see how she could handle the rest herself. If she failed, then she had to do all meals and snacks with us. Again, we were the bad guys, the food police.

Alicia was now a sophomore in high school. She quit Cheer but continued hanging out with friends. She began cutting class and not doing homework. This was something that we never had dealt with. We decided that grades were not going to be the focus but staying in school was. Then in January we realized that she was clinically depressed. She didn't care about anything. She quit hanging out and stayed home and slept a lot. The therapist was very nice but not working for her.

In February, we were finally able to get her in with a therapist that Stanford had recommended way back in June of the prior year, but who was booked up at the time. Alicia has been with her ever since and she is probably the person that Alicia trusts the most. Alicia also saw a psychiatrist and was put on Prozac. This was to be a temporary solution to help with the depression and she was only on it for about fifteen months. We now had a good team for Alicia: her psychologist, psychiatrist and her pediatrician. (We added family therapy a year ago and that has helped tremendously).

Sophomore year was not an easy year. There were a lot of lies and deception. I took it personally and tried to be the parent, i.e., enforcer. I did a bad job at it. Our relationship was not very good. There was a lot of mistrust on both sides and she continued to skip meals and snacks and purge. She remained at 86 or 87 lbs. I remember her pediatrician telling me that we had "at least a couple more years" of this as there has to be a maturity that must take place. I thought that there was no way that I could survive a couple more years. This illness took a toll on my daughter by robbing her of her health, the activities that she loved, her friends, and her life. It robbed her family too. We saw less and less of friends, the topic of conversation was always anorexia, we had to have meals ready and be on a schedule so spontaneity was gone. Our work lives suffered. We slept less and worried constantly. Would she have to go back to the hospital this week or the next? We lived with this disorder hanging over us and we could only hope and pray that one day she would finally slay this monster.

Sophomore year ended and her junior year began. Our communications began to improve and I think Alicia was learning more about herself and beginning to voice her feelings and needs. I think that she was maturing and we were learning. We began having good conversations and hugs and things began to improve in our relationship. The eating disorder was still present. We finally stopped the Ensure drink at lunch time and had her eat something for lunch. That was difficult for her but she did it. We did continue to meet her at home for lunch because she did admit that she would skip lunch otherwise. She began to slide in November and she was hospitalized for the week of Thanksgiving. Instead of the roomful of friends that came when she was hospitalized in her freshman year, there were only one or two friends that came by to see her. The friends were dropping off. This illness was too much for them.

The good news was that she was kind and thoughtful to the staff and apologized to the nurse that she threatened to strangle with the feeding tube. She ate what she was supposed to. It was also right after this that she realized that she was blowing her chance to go away to college. She was beginning to seriously think about a future. She decided to work harder at school. I always wondered if she ever realized how hard this illness had made it for her brain to function when it was so deprived of nutrition. The fact that she did as well as she did with such a low body weight was amazing. I know that my daughter is very bright. I don't think she realizes just how bright she is. The fact that she is looking to go away to college and was trying to work in that direction was a huge step forward. I tried to get her to consider Middle College for her senior year as I felt she would be happier in that environment and out of the high school environment. She decided to stay at the high school.

Academically Alicia did well, but she was not involved in any activities and her friends were very involved in theirs. This was painful for her and it was very painful for a parent to watch. She said it best to me one night when she was in tears - that she used to be so popular and had so many friends and everyone knew her, but now they walked by her and didn't even acknowledge her. She ended up with a few friends that were not healthy for her, or had their own insecurities, or with kids that had their own issues and were kind of separate from the group. It breaks my heart to see what she lost and how she will look back on these three years. It has been a learning year for us, as parents, also. We have gone the full circle of emotions from disbelief to fear, sadness, helplessness, anger and even rage. We cling to life with hope. Hope for Alicia's full recovery and hope that one day life will go back to "normal", where the word anorexia is not a focus in our lives.

Alicia has grown in her ability to verbalize her feelings and that has been absolutely wonderful. She is kind and thoughtful and caring toward us. She has wonderful insights and great observations about people and situations. She has matured so much. We have grown as parents too. As parents of an anorexic, we have learned that we can only love her and support her at this point. She has the knowledge and support for what she needs to do to recover fully. The ball is in her court as to whether she makes use of these tools. We can't be "food police" or decide how she is going to get better. She still struggles, but she is at the highest weight that she has ever been since the problem began. I strongly believe that she will continue to work on recovery and on getting her life back. We can't do it for her. I think a big turning point is when the person can get good and angry with their eating disorder and decide that it has taken away more than it has given. I hope that one day my daughter can put this all behind her and not have to deal with this monster the rest of her life.

I do know that I will always love Alicia no matter what. She is an amazingly strong and wonderful daughter. We are committed to supporting her fight against the illness. This disorder can take over a family's life. In fact, it can zap the life out of every member of the family, not just the person suffering. Anorexia doesn't just try to destroy the life of the person that has it; it also tries to destroy their families. My husband and I forgot how to enjoy life and look to our future. Our daughter, no doubt felt the same way. No wonder she became depressed. We are realizing that it is time to get on with our lives and start to heal. After three-and-a-half long years, we are beginning to see the light at the end of the tunnel. We continue to keep our faith and hope for her full recovery. We know that she can do this and that she will continue to rise to the challenges that come along the road to recovery.

LEAH, AGE 17

So the funny thing about eating disorders is that the one characteristic that makes each specific case universal is that if you ask the afflicted person about their childhood, many of them will say the same thing, "I was such a happy child!" It is almost as though if a child is too happy, the eating disorder will come find them. Penetrate them. Poison them. Drain every ounce of innocence and life that child once had. Or at least, that is what happened to me.

I grew up in a perfect family. At least that's what we pretended to be. Both my parents were high -powered lawyers. My father, famous for his work, would go on business trips regularly and was rarely home. My mother also loved her work, in fact she loved her work so much, parenting took the back seat. As a result, my sister and I grew up with nannies.

My father always drank a lot. However, until I got to middle school I thought it was completely normal. When I entered fourth grade, my father got a promotion which entailed a huge bonus but also caused him to drink more from the stress. My dad would scream at my sister and me and sometimes get very violent. Rachel, my older sister, learned at young age to run away. When Dad began to drink she just left. But when she left, she also left me alone with my dad. As a result, I was usually his target.

When Rachel entered high school she began to play sports, which enabled her to stay out until my dad would either black out or pass out. As I entered middle school, I became more reserved, more closed off. I felt self -conscious all the time. When my Dad would drink he would yell at me telling me how "fat" and "worthless" I was. I felt my self worth and my weight were somehow intertwined. By this time I felt so helpless. I thought, "Wow. Am I really too fat and ugly for even a parent to love?"

When he would hurt me, it was at least attention. My mother was never home. She would always be at work until at least 9 at night, sometimes later. So I didn't see her much. I always wondered why she didn't protect me. I was terrified. I felt as if I wasn't worthy of her protection and therefore was a bad daughter. After my Dad's frequent "episodes," he would always take me shopping thinking this made up for what he'd done. He would somehow rationalize his abuse. After he hurt me he always told me how much he loved me, and how sorry he was, and that it would never happen again. Being naïve and 12, I of course believed him.

In middle school I was very tall for my age. I felt so awkward. I was a dancer, and was surrounded by a bunch of 5'0, 85-pound girls! I was 5'7 by 7th grade. In 8th grade, my Dad's abuse became completely unbearable. His episodes were happening multiple times a week. I felt so ashamed and scared. My mother told me I was being over-dramatic and needed to learn he was only showing me love in a "different" way.

In January of 8th grade I began dieting. I started slow. I began eating salad for lunch and dinner. I felt so in control! I began losing weight and everyone around me told how amazing I looked. I wanted to lose more! However, dieting stopped working, so I found bulimia. At the time, I didn't think I was bulimic. I honestly thought I was obese and was going to die unless I lost weight, and fast! By the end of 8th grade I was down to just under 100 pounds. My close friends attempted to confront me, but I denied everything.

High school was a huge culture shock. Transitioning from a small private school to a big public school was definitely a change for me. I had many new friends, and was getting lots of new attention from boys. My best friend,

Bryn, told my mother about my eating disorder in September of that year. My mother was completely shocked! She had no idea, until she finally took a real look at me. For a few months, she tiptoed around the idea of getting me help, until my sister and aunt told her how sick I looked. In January, she sent me to Tonja, my therapist. For the next two years Tonja and I worked together. It took a good year before I trusted her enough to be honest.

During my sophomore year, I began spinning out of control. I went through a hard break up in January of that year, and it made my eating disorder worse. I felt powerless and unloved. I began purging everything I ate. I started puking up blood, my hair was falling out, and I began fainting. My parents were furious with me. They couldn't understand why I couldn't just quit.

Finally, in March of that year, I told a tutor what was happening at home and about my father's history of alcoholism and abuse. She called my parents in. My Dad began going to AA meetings, seeing a therapist himself, and going to anger management classes. For the first time I thought there was a possibility of things being okay. However, I was wrong. My Dad quit going to the meetings, therapist, and classes after about a month. However, he was no longer hurting me, which helped a lot.

Junior year was an intense year for me. During that year, I began partying, hard.. In February I was raped. I completely lost it. I felt stolen. Betrayed and broken. I felt alone and dirty all the time. I just stopped eating, and became very ill. I honestly just wanted to die. I thought, "How could I possibly be worth loving after all I have done?" I felt the abuse, the eating disorder, the rape, and my father's alcoholism were all my fault. Finally, I put all my faith in recovery. I was completely exhausted. I just couldn't keep living like I was, and I knew I was going to die if I didn't start taking recovery seriously.

I have just finished my senior year of high school. I have not purged in over six months and I am finally learning to accept who I am. I will be honest. There are days where it is hard. Excruciatingly hard. There are days where I want to curl up in a ball and forget everything recovery has taught me, but I have learned that I can no longer go back. For me it is a life and death situation.

I no longer blame myself for everything that has happened but I am slowly learning to take responsibility for how I handle others. I cannot control my family, and my eating disorder is most definitely not going to help me do it. My father is still an alcoholic, however I am bigger than what has happened to me. For so long my eating disorder was my entire life, but for the first time I have a life of my own. I will be attending a LMU in the fall. Recovery gave me my life back. I'm not saying recovery is easy. It's a long, hard, scary road, which involves facing your demons head on, but hey ..anything is possible.

JUSTIN, AGE 24

My sister, Tina, is 20 years old. She was diagnosed with Anorexia a few months ago. Her problems started a year ago when she broke up with her boyfriend. I hadn't seen her for a few months and when she came to visit me, she looked incredibly thin. She told me that she was working out a lot. She was running 7-10 miles a day and on top of that, doing aerobics at the gym. She was eating "healthy" which meant salads. She continued to decrease in size. I was worried, but she convinced me and my parents that she was fine and there was nothing to worry about.

The next time I saw her was a few months later. She looked like a skeleton. I knew at that point something was very wrong. I shared my concerns and my observations with her. I encouraged her to get help, but she continued to deny having a problem. My whole family knew something was terribly wrong, but we didn't know what to do. We all felt extremely helpless. We wanted to support her, but we knew that she had her own life in college away from all of us. We did not see her all the time and could not observe what she was doing to herself on a daily basis. This made it extremely hard to confront her and express our concerns.

Gradually, her eating disorder got worse and fortunately she called our mom and admitted that she thought she might have a problem. She was constantly cold. She had no energy. She couldn't concentrate at school and eventually had to leave. This was extremely hard for her since she attended a prestigious school where she was a straight A student and very involved in extra-curricular activities. She said she was having a nervous breakdown and needed our mother to come get her. My mom went down to her school and it was at that time that she finally admitted she was not eating. She was eating no more than 500 calories per day and exercising between three to five hours per day. She had also started to throw up when she did eat. She was scared to eat alone. She was scared to eat with others. Her fears were intense and she did not want to gain weight.

My sister is incredibly smart. She has always been a hard worker and has done well academically, socially, and occupationally. When she developed an eating disorder, things did not come as easy to her. She had a hard time focusing in school and going to class. She became more isolated and avoided her friends. She did continue to spend time with her boyfriend, but her anxiety level was high and she constantly felt like she was not good enough when she was around him and his friends. Everything she did seemed to consume more of her energy and it was as if she went through life with a 60 pound weight on her back. She wanted to remain thin, but realized it was taking a toll on her mind and her body.

Tina is different from most people who struggle with an eating disorder. She was the one who sought out help and had great motivation to change. She had an initial evaluation with an eating disorder specialist. The specialist took one look at her and was immediately concerned. Tina was pale, lethargic, skeletally thin, and lightheaded. In addition, her hair was thin and she was wearing layers of clothing on a warm day. The specialist insisted that she go directly to a medical doctor to check for medical instability.

At the doctor's appointment later that day, Tina was admitted to the hospital for low heart rate, low temperature, and unstable blood pressure. She stayed at the hospital for four weeks. She did not want to admit that she had a true problem because she did not want to be labeled. Even though she was the one who asked for help due to her understanding of a serious condition, she resisted the label of an eating disorder. My sister has always been the one in the family without problems. I have had my fair share of problems and the attention and focus that comes with them. She has always tried to avoid such problems by being the "perfect child." She succeeded in this until now. Her shame and embarrassment were unnecessary due to the loving and supportive family we have. However, nonetheless, she wanted to pretend like this was not a true illness.

Tina felt so strongly about this that she tried to convince all the doctors, nurses, and social workers that she would recover on her own and did not need any therapeutic intervention. Luckily my whole family understood the severity of the situation. Although they stuck by her and remained supportive, they also firmly told her that she would participate in outpatient treatment or she would be admitted to a residential program. The hospital recommended the residential program due to her severe condition. However, Tina refused this and decided to enter into outpatient therapy. She worked with an individual therapist weekly. She refused to attend family therapy meetings. However, my mother, father, and I sought support from a family therapist. We wanted to do the right thing and not cause her any steps backward in her treatment and recovery.

I played a large role in her recovery. Tina began eating with me at every meal. I always had to eat more than she or she would freak out and stop eating. She needed to be the one eating less food. If she had more than I she would see herself as fat and worthless. I gained a lot of weight in an attempt to help her gain weight. I would talk to her about her thoughts regarding the illness and she said that she was driven to look perfect in an attempt to alleviate her sadness over the breakup with her boyfriend. She opened up to me about her anxiety and distress and the pressure she puts on herself to be perfect. The good student, the good daughter, the good girlfriend, the good worker were all roles she adopted. Nobody else put these pressures on her, they came from within.

Tina did indeed gain weight. She was motivated to get well so she would not be labeled. Maybe this is not the best motivation, but it worked. She gained some weight pretty quickly and was allowed by her doctors to exercise again. However, since then, she has dropped out of therapy and stopped attending her doctors' appointments and meetings with her nutritionist. She is convinced that she is recovered and can handle the illness on her own. I am less certain. I do believe that when my sister sets her mind to accomplish something, she can indeed accomplish it. However, I am very aware of how aggressive an eating disorder can be and the road to recovery is not easy. I will always be there for my sister. I love her very much. She is very special and important to me. If she has setbacks, I will encourage her to get back on track and re-enter therapy. She is an intelligent, strong-willed individual for whom I have the utmost respect, and I will always be there to lend support.

It is not easy being the sibling of a family member who has an eating disorder. You are not the parent who can make decisions around treatment and recovery. You are not the person going through the personal struggle. You are an onlooker who loves and cares for the sick family member and often feels helpless. However, I have learned that the role of the sibling is incredibly important. You are the person who can encourage, support, and motivate to change. You are the person who can distract from the distress of the eating problem and build your sister/brother up. It is not easy to see your family member sick. It is not easy to think about what could happen if she does not get well. It is a great feeling to do something to help her and support her. I took Tina to the movies, the beach, and on walks. Anything to get her mind off the anxiety produced by the eating disorder. You can make a difference. Your sibling needs you.

10

APPENDIX A

INDIVIDUAL THERAPY
Cognitive Behavioral Therapy (CBT)

CHALLENGING IRRATIONAL/NEGATIVE THOUGHTS

Derived from Cognitive Behavioral Therapy, a wonderful starting intervention is to help the individual make the connection between thoughts, feelings, and behavior (ED). Start by identifying an antecedent event that leads to the cyclical process which ultimately ends in ED.

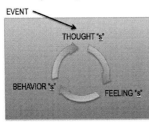

Recognition of irrational/negative thoughts can bring incredible insight into the individual's process and recovery.

Cycling Process

ALTERNATIVE BEHAVIORS

1. **Purpose:** I strongly believe that Restricting/Binging/ Purging is a coping mechanism. It is a way to manage uncomfortable, distressing feelings that seem unmanageable. Therefore, every treatment plan should include an exploration of alternative behaviors. Increasing the child's coping mechanisms can ultimately lead to a decrease in the ED behavior.

2. **Steps necessary for success:**

❋ First, one must figure out the reason (Why?) behind the ED behavior. For example, "I purge to relieve tension."

❋ Second, one must validate to the child that the ED behavior is fulfilling a specific need. For example, "You purge because it relieves tension and stress and makes you feel better."

❋ Third, one can then explore with the child what behaviors could potentially fulfill that same need. For example, "What else could you do to relieve tension and stress and feel better?"

❋ Remember, if the substitute/alternative behavior does not fulfill the same need, the child will be left feeling uncomfortable and in distress and will continue to have the urge to Restrict/Binge/Purge. **The alternative behavior must fulfill the same need.**

❋ Make a list of at least five alternative behaviors. Realize that this is a trial and error process. Some behaviors may work and some may not. The goal is to give the child options when feeling the urge to restrict/binge/

purge. Remember many kids believe that their only option is to engage in these behaviors.

WARNING:

❋ In the beginning, alternative behaviors may not provide the same relief that the eating disorder does.

❋ What these alternative behaviors will provide is a way to experience genuine emotion, for better or for worse, which they will learn to better cope with through more positive means.

11

APPENDIX B

INDIVIDUAL THERAPY - Insight-Oriented Work

I cover the specific topics listed below during treatment sessions with my patients to help them better understand the reasons behind their eating disorder. Many of these topics come from Wendy Lader and Karen Conterio's book, *Self Harm*. However, others are based on interventions utilized by narrative therapists nationwide.

Usually, I cover these topics in a verbal dialogue; however, some of my patients have difficulty with verbal self-expression. Therefore, if this is case, I will address these topics in the form of written assignment and review. I ask my patient to write about these topics and then bring in her written work to share with me. Sometimes she reads to me what she has written and other times she wants me to read her work and then discuss it with her.

I have found that journaling can be incredibly thera-peutic for individuals who struggle with eating disorders. Whether they are good with verbal self-expression or not, written expression tends to help the individual organize her thoughts and feelings, increase insight into her problems, and make realizations about her unhealthy behavior. Journaling is an activity that is safe and constructive. It can open the window of opportunity between urges to restrict/binge/purge and participating in the actual behavior.

It is important to keep in mind that not everybody likes to write. I encourage every patient I see to journal because I recognize the value in it. I always have journals on hand in my office that I offer to new patients. However, if I have a patient who is highly resistant to writing, I do not push this mode of expression. If she struggles verbally and is resistant to writing, then I try to engage her in another cre-ative way (i.e., art therapy, music therapy, drama therapy, etc.) The goal is not how to cover the topics, but simply to cover them in some way to help gain insight into her prob-lems. Below I have listed many of the treatment topics that I address with my patients.

SPECIFIC TREATMENT TOPICS

1. Tell Your Story: This is a type of autobiography. The goal is to describe, in as much detail as possible, dif-ferent events in your life, from early childhood memo-ries to the present. This may include topics such as

family (family dynamics, emotional climate, relationships), peer group (friends, significant others, relationships/conflicts), academic history, medical history, psychiatric history (including eating problems, substance abuse, etc.), employment history, leisure activities (hobbies, talents, special interests), hardships or losses, trauma, etc.

2. Personal Identity: This helps the individual explore the way in which she sees herself. I often distinguish between how the person sees herself on the inside versus the outside. I also explore her thoughts about how others perceive her on these two levels. The person should identify personal strengths and weaknesses and how these affect her coping abilities, relationships, and self-esteem. The patient should include thoughts about gender, race, and ethnicity. Positive thoughts about any of these can help build self-esteem. Negative thoughts can contribute to self-hatred and self-destruction. The patient should also include the different roles she plays in her life. Varying roles may have varying influences on the patient. This is worth exploration and discovery.

3. Role Models: The most influential female and/or the most influential male in the patient's life could serve as a role model for the patient and aid in his or her recovery process. It is important for the therapist to explore what type of positive influences this person has on the patient. If there are only negative influences, process why this individual has been chosen as a role model.

4. Thoughts and Feelings Associated with the Eating Disorder: This topic helps the patient develop greater insight into the things that lead to eating disorder behavior. Remember with knowledge and awareness comes the power to change. *Note: I pay attention to 'all or nothing' thinking. Often patients who struggle with an eating disorder do not view things in shades of gray. I try to help the individual break through this type of thinking and expand her insight.

5. Building Relationships: This topic helps the patient recognize what it takes to build a non-superficial relationship. This may be a foreign concept to the person. Eating disorders often isolate the patient from others instead of drawing them closer. They can destroy relationships or make them much more conflictual. Many patients report having conflictual relationships which leaves them feeling empty, lonely, and/or distrustful of others. This lowers self-esteem and deserve level which can lead to further eating disorder behaviors.

6. Conflictual Relationships: This topic is also insight oriented. If the patient can identify the person or people with whom he or she is in conflict and why, then the patient can begin to explore ways in which to handle these conflicts differently (especially if he or she is using the eating disorder as the primary coping mechanism).

7. Self-Expression: This is a very important topic. I encourage my patient to explore ways in which she

verbally expresses herself (if at all). I have found that many patients struggle with verbal self-expression. Instead, they express themselves through what they do with food. Exploration of why there is a lack of verbal self-expression is the key in helping the patient utilize this tool. For example, many patients talk about their fear of disappointing others or angering others with their words. This fear keeps them from verbalizing their pain, which in turn builds tension and leads to restricting/binging/purging. I process with my patient their fears, whether or not they are realistic, and what they can do about them. It is important for the patient to begin to practice ways in which she can communicate her thoughts and feelings to others. This can be extremely empowering for her. I have found that with increased verbal self-expression there is often a large decrease in eating disorder behavior.

8. Critical Life Events: This topic allows individuals to focus specifically on any trauma or loss that they have experienced in their lives. Included should be fantasies of revenge and alternative outcomes as well as realistic ways to feel more empowered and less victimized. Pay close attention to self-blame and/or guilt. These are often pre-cursors to eating disorder behavior. Individuals who blame themselves or experience guilt due to trauma or loss often feel a need to punish themselves and use restricting/binging/purging as their means to cope.

9. Taking Care of Oneself: This topic helps the patient explore ways in which she can self-soothe other than

through the absence or use of food. Some patients do not know of any other self-soothing techniques. I often need to help my patients explore what these could be. Also I pay close attention to my patient's deserve level. Many patients do not believe they are deserving of nurturance. Building self-esteem and building deserve level are two main goals in therapy for the person with an eating disorder.

10. Summary of Progress: This topic can reinforce the awareness that has been built up in treatment and the changes made. As a therapist, I often utilize the intervention of "summarizing progress." I think reviewing the positive changes a person has made can help to reinforce these changes. Many of my patients have great difficulty giving themselves credit for their hard work in treatment. This topic allows that to occur. Having patients summarize their progress seems to reinforce their changes even more because they are more likely to own (internalize) what they say.

11. Miracle Question: This is a narrative therapy technique. It allows the patient to imagine what her life would be like without an eating disorder. In a detailed description, the patient reveals how the loss of this behavior in exchange for healthier, less destructive coping mechanisms will change their mood, activities, relationships, thought process, etc. It is a tool used to instill hope, motivation, and commitment to change.

12. The Funeral: This is a way to say good-bye to their eating disorder. I encourage patients to become creative with this powerful topic. I have had patients write

eulogies or plant flowers/trees. I even had a patient who conducted an actual funeral service with friends and families in attendance. Remember that eating disorders often become part of the patient's identity. Therefore, saying good-bye to this act can be very difficult. Giving the patient this opportunity can be very empowering and opens new pathways for self-definition/identity.

13. My Future: This final topic allows the patient to have an action plan in place. This action plan, in and of itself, can alleviate anxiety and help the patient be more constructive. This plan may be created for daily, weekly or monthly use. The patient will need to decide what she needs in order to be most successful in living without the eating disorder. The patient should create reasonable goals for herself that are attainable to reinforce success. These goals do not have to focus on eating disorders. In fact, they should begin to branch away from this problem. For example, a goal might revolve around school or work or becoming involved with a certain activity/hobby that is of interest to the person. It may include straightening out finances, finding trusted others to support her in times of distress or planning a vacation. In any case, the goals should help the individual create new ways (more positive ways) to define her, build self-esteem and self-confidence, and widen her support system. Once the patient has achieved these goals, she can create new ones.

Often parents are interested in talking with their child about their treatment. This is not a bad thing to do, but if you choose to discuss their treatment with them, please make note of the following:

❋ Avoid power struggles when trying to obtain information

❋ Don't minimize the eating disorder behavior

❋ Don't let others (including medical doctors) deny the seriousness of the problem

❋ Don't encourage/give permission for the use of other "acting out" behaviors (i.e. over exercise, etc.)

❋ Keep your own emotions in check

❋ Trust your instincts

❋ Remember Eating Disorders are sneaky, manipulative, and lie. They do not see things clearly and will try to avoid intervention every chance they get.

This last bullet point may confuse you. I do in fact mean that "eating disorders," - not your child - are sneaky, manipulative, and lie. Eating disorders cause your child to do and say things that she would never have done or said before the onset of the illness. The thoughts that creep into a child's mind who is suffering from an eating disorder are very different from the thoughts of those who do not have this problem. The constant fear of gaining weight and looking fat will change your child's motivations and actions drastically. Several examples of this are shared in the inspiring stories chapter in this book.

Published by FastPencil
http://www.fastpencil.com